Sensei, Mentor, Teacher, Coach

Praise for Sensei, Mentor, Teacher, Coach …

"How refreshing! Finally a book that will actually move the needle in closing the leadership skills gap found in all aspects of our society. This book is engaging from the introduction to the last page, it is practical so you can immediately put it into action, and it is going to help those leaders who are in the trenches and making a difference every day.

"Much effort and resources are invested in developing business strategies, getting senior management on board, and driving strategies top down. We also spend a lot of time building grassroots support for those strategies so that we have bottom-up support in the trenches. But, what we often miss is what I call "winning the middle," earning the trust and support of those middle managers, and thought and opinion leaders who make or break our companies and institutions. This book addresses this gap head on.

"It is easy to read and quick to put into action. It's a winner and going to help a lot of people!" – **Dan Roberts**, CEO and President, Ouellette & Associates Consulting; Author of *Unleashing the Power of IT* and *Confessions of a Successful CIO*

❖❖❖

"This spoke to my heart. This book personifies my beliefs about leadership and leading. It is truly exceptional how the authors pulled so many known concepts into a string of actions. The "Tasks of the Week" are the perfect guideline to train oneself to be a better leader through exercises. I am going to recommend this to everyone within my company as well as my professional and private circles." – **Dawn Tiura Evans**, President and CEO, Sourcing Interests Group

❖❖❖

"Kane and Wilder have brought together time proven individual development and personnel management techniques, wrapping them in a historical context and quotes that help bring home their unique point of view. Whether you are a *sensei*, coach, or simply a manager, you will find useful techniques in this book that allow you, and those who interact with you, to grow." – **John Lytle**, Director, Information Services Group

❖❖❖

"Wilder and Kane have plenty of experience with leadership in all aspects of life and it shows. Deftly mixing greater overarching concepts with pointed and pithy anecdotes from a wide variety of sources, every page has practical advice and words of wisdom. I especially liked the "Little Life Secrets" and "Coach Tips" for their ways of taking more-abstract ideas and bringing them to life for me, and found the exercises scattered throughout interesting as ways to approach situations in novel yet realistic manners." – **Bruce A. Ritzen**, JD

❖❖❖

"A fine book in which the authors have succeeded not only in bringing together a range of teachings for the modern world, but in which they provide practical, action oriented advice that can be referred to over and over again. Not just advice on how to be a better leader in business, but on how to be a better person in life." – **Howard Davies**, Managing Director, Alsbridge Consulting

❖❖❖

"Easy, quick read, packed with practical information for new leadership and middle management roles. This is a book you will dog ear for quick reference and keep on your desk or in your pocket." – **Paul Becker**, Transition and Optimization Leader

❖❖❖

"I'm at the age where I tend to look backward over my life. When reading any form of self-help, self-evaluation or general advice for living, I reflect on how the advice would have been useful in previous situations as opposed to future ones. I tend to be very comfortable with myself, regardless of how comfortable others may be with me. It's a blessing and a curse. It is with this perspective that I thoroughly enjoyed Kane and Wilder's newest book.

"In almost every chapter I found advice, stories, and examples that made me think, "Yep, that does work," and "If I had taken that approach at the time, things would probably have gone a whole lot smoother." Now that I am well into the "I'm too old to learn new stuff" phase of life, acknowledging even to myself that there would have been a better way of approaching a problem is nothing short of revelation.

"This is a book I will suggest to my own children and grandchildren. It is also a book that I recommend, as I have with other Kane/Wilder books, as reading material made available in schools. Insights provided can help bosses, teachers, and coaches as well as employees, students, and team members perform at the 110% we all hear about. It's about increasing your contribution to, influence on, and satisfaction with reaching any stated objective.

"Never wanting to leave well enough alone, I will admit to wishing that more of the book emphasized humor as a way of making friends and influencing people. I guess I just like funny stories better now than actually having to learn stuff. Despite my obstinacy I acquired invaluable information from this book and am confident that you will too. Highly recommended!" – **Michael Murphy**, Director, Bellevue WA School Board

❖❖❖

"I really liked the book. The layout with tips and secrets is very helpful. I was impressed with the number of examples that the authors used; especially the breadth of examples—using history, sports, and business as well as their personal experiences. It doesn't matter what part of life you walk in, this book has examples that anyone can relate to. Just having concepts with no examples does not give people concrete ways of applying them, whereas just having tactics without the big picture causes people to miss the essence and foundation of what leadership even is. This excellent book has both." – **Dr. Letha Joye Jepson**, PhD, Leadership & Change

❖❖❖

"A superb book that covers all aspects of leadership in a simple, structured and accessible way. This book provides a great resource for all leaders, regardless of whether your leadership role is that of middle manager, small business owner, sports coach, or any other position where you are responsible for the organization, success and wellbeing of others. The underlying principles of leadership are covered brilliantly and the innovative "Task of the Week" sections give the reader the opportunity to put these principles into practice immediately. The complete package!" – **Iain Abernethy**, Author, Martial Arts Instructor, and Small Business Owner

❖❖❖

"This book represents a realistic approach to facilitating changes within middle management. It helps to identify what a manager could and could not do within the corporate environment. I particularly like the approach to sighting the theory, the practical application, and the steps you have to take to make changes. This is a practical book for making positive changes." – **Vard B. Wallace, III**, Adjunct Professor, Northwest University

❖❖❖

"*Sensei, Mentor, Teacher, Coach* is an excellent primer for new and aspiring managers. I was pleasantly surprised to find in one source lessons and management techniques that I learned over a 25 year career. Had I had this book when I was starting out I would have been ahead of my peers and much wiser for it." – **Kathy Rudy**, Partner, Information Services Group

❖❖❖

Sensei, Mentor, Teacher, Coach

Powerful Leadership for Leaderless Times

Kris Wilder and Lawrence A. Kane

Stickman Publications
2147 SW 115th Street
Burien, WA 98146

Copyright © 2013 by Kris Wilder & Lawrence A. Kane
Cover art, design and interior layout by Kamila Miller

All rights reserved. Reproduction of any part or the whole of this work in any form without prior written permission from the copyright owners is prohibited. No part of this publication may be reproduced, stored in or introduced into a retrieval system, or transmitted in any form or by any means (electronic, mechanical, photocopying, recording, or otherwise), without authorization. To request the authors' consent to reproduce any portions of this work please contact the authors through their website at www.westseattlekarate.com.

ISBN-13: 978-1495407161
ISBN-10: 1495407160

Disclaimer

Information in this book is distributed "As Is," without warranty. Nothing in this document constitutes a legal opinion nor should any of its contents be treated as such. Neither the authors nor the publisher shall have any liability with respect to information contained herein. Further, neither the authors nor the publisher have any control over or assume any responsibility for websites or external resources referenced in this book.

Acknowledgements

Kane has had the great fortune of working for some amazing managers, Mike Mesick, Mary Scheyer, Steve Schreck, Dan Grudt, and Susan Gellatly to name a few, but the one who taught him the most about leadership was Mike Luxenberg. Lux was tough, but fair, courageous and inspirational, yet what set him apart was mentorship. He not only demonstrated the right behaviors, but also explained the reasons why. After retiring from Boeing, he continued to be an adviser, meeting regularly for several years to act as a sounding board and offer advice. A truly stellar individual, his guidance helped inspire this book.

Many people have made differences in Wilder's life, impressions made that sometimes manifest long after they were cast. Many martial artists, many coaches, many bosses, and many, many moments from a tight and extended family that knew the value of love in all its capacities, all are blessings. Two moments stand out. When asked what he wanted to do, Wilder replied, "Make a difference." Then Paccar (Kenworth Trucks) Director of Government Relations Jack McCrae said, "You can do that with your next door neighbor, you don't need to be here (Paccar) to do that." And, Wilder's Godfather, Alan Wall, who told him, "Never chase the dollar."

Paul Becker, John Lytle, and Bruce Ritzen reviewed the draft manuscript, gave us discerning feedback, and helped improve the quality of this work. Thanks guys! Your insight is very much appreciated. Any residual imperfections are our own.

CONTENTS

FOREWORD	v
INTRODUCTION	vii
HOW TO USE THIS BOOK	ix
CREATING LEADERS	1
ESPRIT DE CORPS	9
PROBLEMS ARE NORMAL	21
FLAWED THINKING	33
THINKING BEYOND THE OBVIOUS	59
DON'T FEAR EXPECTATIONS	69
CONTEXT IS CRITICAL	71
TACKLING INSURMOUNTABLE CHALLENGES	81
THE TURNING POINT	89
BREAK IT DOWN, BUILD IT UP	97
THREEFOLD MISSION STATEMENT	103
PLAN – DO – CHECK – ACT	119
CROSS-POLLINATION	127
IMAGE	133
THE RIGHT WORDS	141
BRAIN TYPING	151
RECOGNIZING EFFORT	161
MORE THAN JUST TECHNIQUES	171
DOING THE RIGHT THING	183
PASSIO	193
CONCLUSION	201
BIBLIOGRAPHY	203
END NOTES	207
ABOUT THE AUTHORS	215
OTHER WORKS BY THE AUTHORS	219

Foreword

Colonel Anthony A. Wood, USMC (ret)

Currently an inspirational speaker and leadership consultant, Colonel Anthony A. Wood is best known for his heroic role in the evacuation of Saigon during the Vietnam War. He organized a group of 100 American civilian volunteers who assumed great personal risk to remain without protection and evacuate over 5,000 persons from the collapsing capital to the safety of waiting Marine helicopters. When he retired from the Marine Corps in June 1998, he was the only Colonel or Captain in any of the United States armed services to have twice been decorated with the nation's second highest award, the Distinguished Service Medal. He also earned the Legion of Merit, the Bronze Star with Combat V, the Meritorious Service Medal, the Joint Service Commendation Medal (multiple awards), the Humanitarian Assistance Medal, and the Combat Action Ribbon (multiple awards). After his military career Colonel Wood became the Director of Applied Research for the CAD Research Center at California Polytechnic State University as well as the Vice President/COO and Partner of CDM Technologies, an advanced software development company. He continues to serve in a variety of capacities on boards. His website is www.colonelanthonywood.com.

I owe a large debt to Dan Roberts, author of *Unleashing the Power of IT*, for it was he who introduced me to the authors of *Sensei, Mentor, Teacher, Coach* and suggested that I might wish to draft a foreword for this amazing work. At the time I was preparing for a leadership presentation to the Society for Information Management, SIM, featuring the civilian heroes whose courage was critical to successfully executing the risky evacuation of Saigon in the spring of 1975. As a Marine officer for more than thirty years and, more recently Vice President/COO and corporate partner in an IT company for fifteen, I remember thinking just after Roberts' call that I would likely be familiar with much of what this book contained and that I could provide a solid overview and at the same time endorse a fresh approach to the tried and true sinews of leadership. So much for my hubris and overconfidence…

Among the thousands of books on this subject I am amazed that Wilder and Kane have not only found a new approach, but one that makes a real difference. Leaders and mentors of all stripes should read this book for what it is—a martial arts manual on leading that shoves us face-to-face with the "how to" of developing, strengthening, and nurturing the sinews and muscles of real leadership. Senior leaders will see it as an invaluable resource for mentoring those who must follow them. Mid-level leaders will find in it a wealth of practical advice for improving their capabilities to serve their co-workers, their companies, and their communities. On the other hand, would be-leaders and self-centered careerists have real reason to fear exposure as others absorb the book's not so subtle message that leading is both a privilege and an opportunity to serve, and carries with it the responsibility to continuously hone the skills that enable effective service.

Even the style of the prose in *Sensei, Mentor, Teacher, Coach* drives home the message. It is straightforward and in-your-face, refreshingly free of literary artistry and self-congratulatory passages. This combination of honesty, thoroughness, and practicality gives the book its power.

Those who already consider themselves experts on what makes a good leader are in for some real surprises. The practical exercises that reinforce each chapter and the "Tips" framed to emphasize the main points are pure gold. If you step out of your skin and try a few of these application exercises, you'll be doubly rewarded with a healthy shot of humility combined with valuable new insights. Try it, I did.

There is no excess fat in the manual Wilder and Kane have produced. The authors' eyes never wander from their subject to contemplate the effect they are creating. This transparency in style conveys the message without diverting us. The honesty, simplicity, and modesty give the book extraordinary power. The exercise structure drawn from martial arts grants a logical and practical approach. Throughout, the understated message is that our role as leaders is to serve and, in order to serve well; we have a responsibility to hone the skills that can make us able sensei, mentors, teachers, and coaches.

Anthony A. Wood
Colonel (Ret.), U. S. Marine Corps 1964 –1998
Former Vice President and Partner, CDM Technologies Inc., 1998 – 2011
Dallas Texas, January 2014

Introduction

"We work to become, not to acquire." – Elbert Hubbard[1]

The definers and shapers at the core of any society are the people in the middle, the normal work-a-day folks. No culture or organization can be driven solely by the great executive, the president, or the CEO. Sure, those at the top can craft a vision or architect a strategy, but they cannot simultaneously perform every function necessary to carry it out. To have any real shot at turning vision into reality, those in the middle must do the heavy lifting and lead.

While those at the top cannot shape society alone, a sad fact is that those at the bottom do not have the resources or clout necessary to make any substantive difference either. Consequently it falls to folks in the middle to exercise leadership on a daily basis in order to make their lives, their organizations, and the lives of those around them better.

This book was not written for the 64th floor executive. It is certainly not designed for the homeless and destitute either as day-to-day survival is their hourly charge. This book is, however, created for you, for us, and for others like us, the folks in the middle. We are the engine that makes society and culture what it is or what it can be. To do that, to affect people on a gut-level, to lead, we need to step into the breach where the void of leadership lies and pledge on an everyday basis that we will make others' lives better and in turn improve our own existence and the lives of our loved ones as well.

While leadership *can* stem from authority, being in charge is by no means a prerequisite to lead. The imperative is to set an example that others will wish to follow. Most of us appreciate the fact that effective leaders know how to set high standards for themselves and others, make tough decisions, overcome challenges, share experiences, surround themselves with good people, and fuel performance, yet the obstacle often comes in figuring out how to accomplish such things. That's where this book comes in; it provides tools and information that help you succeed.

So, mentor, teacher, and coach, choose to lead and read on…

The word *sensei* is found in the title of this book, but you might not know what it means. *Sensei* is a Japanese word, commonly translated as "teacher," that literally denotes "one who has come before." The term is often applied to martial arts instructors, particularly those who teach styles that originated in the Nipponese archipelago such as karate or judo, but it can also signify coaches, mentors, and schoolteachers as well. In essence it is anyone who has acquired knowledge, skills, and experience and is willing to share their expertise with others. Sounds a lot like you, right?

While this book is written for you, it is important to understand that leadership really isn't about you. It is about giving back, offering your best to others so that they can find the best in themselves. And, with appreciation, they can pay it forward.

Neither author is perfect by any stretch of the imagination, yet we have done our best to learn from successes and failures alike and will do our utmost to impart our collective wisdom here. As you read through the materials try to take the same tactic. Hold up a small rearview mirror. Learn from the past, but don't dwell on your mistakes. Life is best lived forward with an eye toward the future.

We look to the title of the 1976 Broadway play by Milan Stitt, *The Runner Stumbles*, for a great metaphor. We are all runners in the race of life and we all stumble. It's not a matter of if, but when. The real question becomes one of whether or not we will pick ourselves back up afterward and find our stride. And, in finding our stride, will we come alongside others and encourage them as well. Our conviction is that this book will help you do exactly that.

How to Use This Book

"To improve is to change; to be perfect is to change often."
Winston Churchill[2]

The young man hailed through the open door of the blacksmith's workshop, "The war is over!" The blacksmith glanced up from the sword he was drawing, a process that lengthens and shapes the metal. "Tis?"

"Yes, the king has won. We are victorious."

The blacksmith paused for a second, flipped the sword over on the anvil and started to rework the metal with his hammer. As the blade began to bend the young man asked, "What are you doing to that sword?" The blacksmith said, "It is now a bit for the plow horse."

"But you are the greatest sword-maker in the kingdom!"

"I was," replied the blacksmith. "Now I am the best bit-maker in the land."

Like the blacksmith and his actions, this book is designed to be straightforward, specific, and actionable. Theory is nice, but if you cannot actually do something with new information it becomes "shelfware," quickly forgotten. Consequently we will give you things to think about and actions to take at the end of each chapter to put what you have read to good use.

Our goal is to change the way you see the world and to arm you with knowledge and tools that will help you act on this new perspective. As you progress through the materials, look toward how you can habituate what you have learned, translating it into specific behavioral and communications goals. This will improve your relations with those you are in position to lead. After all, setting an example that others want to follow is the very essence of leadership.

Finally, always prune. Bring the interactions down to the essential and the necessary. Flush the rest.

1

CREATING LEADERS

Seven Essentials of Leadership

"If your actions inspire others to dream more, learn more, do more and become more, you are a leader."
John Quincy Adams[3]

John Quincy Adams, the sixth President of the United States of America, was the son of the second President John Adams and his brilliant wife Abigail. Given the very best education, John Quincy Adams traveled to France as a teen to study and subsequently graduated from Harvard College with a law degree. Later when he wanted to marry a young woman he loved, his father recommended against it, believing that his son had great things in front of him. As it turns out, he did.

Before being elected president, John Quincy Adams was a senator. He also served as ambassador to the Netherlands, Germany, and Russia, as well as Secretary of State. In that capacity he negotiated the Treaty of Ghent ending the war of 1812, helped define the Canadian/United States border, navigated the annexation of Florida from Spain, and helped formulate the Monroe Doctrine. In the electoral tradition of the early 19th century, Adams as Secretary of State was considered the political heir to the Presidency.

As you can see, he was born into a favored position and nurtured along a lofty path from a young age. This brings up the age old argument: are leaders born or made? Both perspectives have merit. Leaders actually are born… and then they are nurtured. But that does not mean that people who are not natural leaders cannot acquire new skills and develop their ability to guide and inspire others.

Here's an example: quiet and unassuming, that was probably the best way you could have described that kid. He was slightly built, weighed virtually nothing, didn't really look people in the eye, smiled quickly, and was generally pleasant. He had been brought into the karate *dojo* (school) by his older brother. He may or may not have wanted to be there, but he put in the effort nonetheless. That's the work ethic he inherited. You see, he came from an immigrant family, one that had escaped horrific oppression from one of the bloodiest regimes in Asia.

As you can imagine they were a no-nonsense household. Mornings came early, days were long and filled with work, and evenings not only served as the time to wrap up the day's events, but also as an opportunity to train the body and mind with more hard work. Both brothers toiled away in the *dojo*, but always hung out in the back, staying out of the limelight. If asked, other students would not point out either brother as a leader, yet whenever they were on the floor all the other students unconsciously emulated their work ethic and perseverance.

Leadership can stem from authority, expertise, or example. With the exception of hierarchical authority, being placed in charge, any example that others want to follow is leadership. While styles vary greatly, traits of good leadership consistently apply to everyone. Leveraging natural charisma is valuable, of course, but it is far less important than behaviors that demonstrate character. Without good character, people will not follow a leader over the long run. The seven essential attributes of leadership include being (1) Consistent, (2) Visionary, (3) Fair, (4) Honest, (5) Courageous, (6) Inspirational, and (7) Productive. Let's elaborate:

1. **Consistent**: earns trust and respect through integrity and dependability. Subordinates, peers, and superiors all know what to expect when interacting with this person. Reliably meets commitments.
2. **Visionary**: conveys a sense of purpose that motivates others. Able to define a strategic direction and success criteria, balance big-picture concerns with day-to-day

issues, set priorities, and continuously course-correct as necessary to achieve results.
3. **Fair**: open-minded. Treats people impartially and objectively. Creates an atmosphere where folks feel comfortable bringing up problems, taking measured risks, and suggesting innovative alternatives.
4. **Honest**: means what they say and says what they mean. Keeps confidences, models integrity, and bounds pursuit of individual objectives with the overall interests of the organization or team.
5. **Courageous**: models confidence. Sees changes as opportunities and demonstrates a willingness to do the right things even when they are not expedient or politically easy.
6. **Inspirational**: builds teams whose performance is greater than the sum of their parts. Celebrates successes and learns from failures, leverages diversity, and sets people up for success.
7. **Productive**: keeps promises and delivers results. Capitalizes on unanticipated opportunities and changing circumstances to meet commitments despite challenges. Continuously improves quality and performance.

Be aware of people in your sphere of influence who set a good example by consistently demonstrating these seven leadership attributes. These individuals show up on time, work diligently, perform well, help others, and are a real asset to the team. Every reasonable effort should be exerted to motivate, train, and retain them. To create leaders you need to help folks acquire the knowledge, skills, and ability for success, give them a chance to lead, and don't let anything (you can influence or control) get in the way of their progress.

Bureaucracy kills momentum. Period. Unfortunately it's also a fact of life in most institutions. We cannot all, or always, avoid bureaucracy. It gets put in place for valid reasons and generally does have some redeeming value, particularly in protecting an organization from irresponsible behaviors, but by its very nature it is the antithesis of innovation and velocity. So, where does that leave you? When you are the decision-maker, make the decision. Do not allow yourself to become paralyzed by burdensome administrivia, excessive analysis, or undue caution or you will let honoring bureaucracy become the de facto behavior.

Juice a project, a game, a new rank in the martial arts. Find the juice and feed the juice. If a game against a highly ranked opponent means that your team has little chance to win, then the juice becomes, "We are as a team going to do some crazy things to give us a shot at victory." Perhaps a new project at work will improve the corporate culture; it's not going to be easy but gives you a chance at achievements that others will want to emulate. A new rank might come with new challenges, which in turn leads to new accomplishments and ever escalating responsibility. Success breeds success, and success is a juice of its own.

Talk about that future. Share your vision of how you see it, your employee's position in that future organization, your player's position on the future of the team, or what the next rank will mean to your student. And do so in concrete terms. There must be actionable items, real titles, real positions, real successes within reach, and you must give the person the right tools to have a legitimate chance at achieving it.

The formula for future talk is: Today + Positive Action = Success (e.g., skill, position, title, or role and everything that comes with it). An example of future talk might sound like this:

> "Susan you are tall enough to play forward on the varsity basketball team. However, you are playing behind a very talented senior who we all know is going to play at the college level. She already has a letter of intent from the U. Learn from her, practice your ball control, and it is likely that you will own that forward position and become our starter next season."

What was heard in this conversation was:

- "You are built for this."
- "You need more experience."
- "Do these two things."
- "You have future."

Today + Positive Action = Position. In this example the coach has not only painted a viable future, but also set Susan up for success in achieving it by explaining exactly what to work on and providing a mentor to help make it happen. The rest is up to her. If she follows through, works hard, and stays on course chances are good that she'll be the starter next year.

The formula of Today + Positive Action = Position may seem to be a simple equation, almost trite, but it is powerful... very powerful. People tend to act in their own enlightened self-interest, yet a common challenge is that we don't always know what our self-interest truly is, what steps are necessary to further our aspirations. That's the power of having a teacher, coach, mentor, or role model, someone who can point the way. Lay out the steps, show the possibilities, explain the reward, and others will latch onto the actions necessary to carry them out.

Sensei, Mentor, Teacher, Coach Tip:

> To create leaders you need to help those around you acquire the knowledge, skills, and abilities they need for success just like President John Adams did for his son John Quincy Adams. And then you need to give them a chance to practice. Find individuals who demonstrate the seven leadership characteristics, give them the tools they need, and a chance to lead.

Action:

You likely already know who your star employee, pupil, or player is, but what about the rest of your team? Are there unsung heroes in your group who just need that one opportunity to shine? One way to find out is to build a simple two-axis table showing "leadership potential" and "experience" on a scale of 1 (low) to 5 (high), and plot the names of everyone in your charge on that page. You can develop discrete criteria for each rating, and should if it will be used in any formal Human Resources process such as succession planning, but even a subjective "gut check" placement should prove illuminating when that level of formality is not required. At a glance you can identify future leaders who need your support.

This process does not directly look at performance. How effectively a person meets their current responsibilities is important, but subject for a different exercise. Our focus here is identifying future leaders so that you can create development opportunities for them to hone their skills.

Here's an example of what the output might look like:

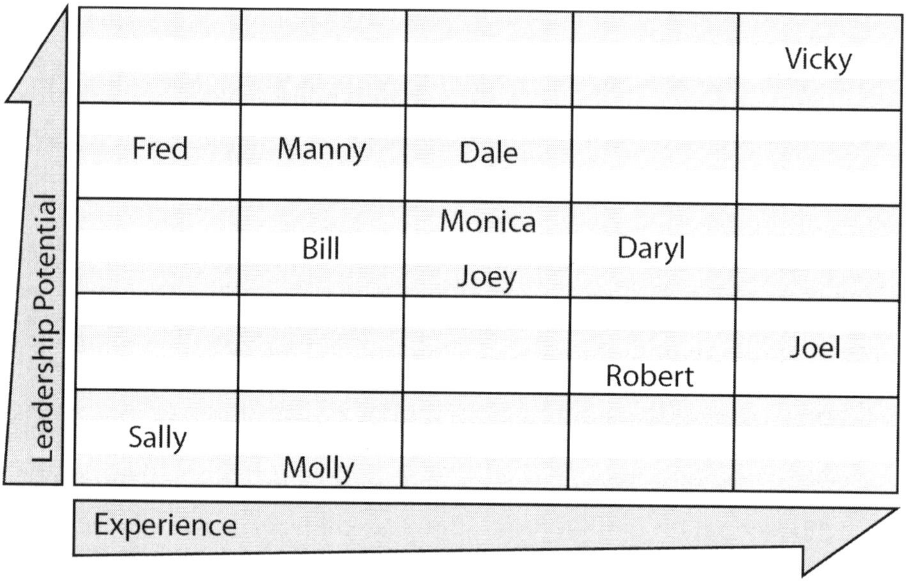
Vicky
Fred
Manny
Dale
Monica
Bill
Daryl
Joey
Joel
Robert
Sally
Molly
Leadership Potential
Experience

In our illustration above Vicky is the current star, but Fred and Manny are likely to become the future if given the chance. Conversely, they are also likely to seek opportunities elsewhere if not provided challenging assignments that help them grow their skills in a timely manner.

It is important to note that people in the lower right segment in our example like Joel or Robert, who have a lot of experience but minimal leadership potential, are not necessarily poor performers or unmanageable employees. They are likely subject matter experts whose capabilities are vital to your organization but who lack the interest or ability to lead. Don't dismiss these individuals out of hand, but rather find ways to leverage their talents for the mutual betterment of themselves and the organization (see Chapter 16, Brain Typing, for more information). These folks often make terrific mentors so long as you can help them see the role as an opportunity and not as a threat, assuring that key technical or process information is safeguarded rather than leaving it as tribal knowledge that is only maintained in somebody's head.

People like Sally or Molly on the lower left segment in our example, on the other hand, may be new hires or internal transfers who need focused training or mentoring in order to learn their responsibilities and get up to speed efficiently. Think more about *who* they need to know than *what* they need to know; tools and processes alone are insufficient in such cases. Provide interactions with subject matter experts to build support networks, insight into the organization's culture so that they will understand how to get things done, and meaningful assignments to hone their skills while doing it. Prudent investments in onboarding will help increase productivity and morale while simultaneously reducing turnover.

Now that you know how to interpret the table, build one for your team. Once complete, choose someone with high leadership potential who has not had a chance to grow their skills recently and find a project that is both a learning experience and an opportunity to make a real difference. It could be as simple as a backup quarterback holding the clipboard and helping with play calling or as complex as a project manager implementing a new Enterprise Resource Planning system (an IT project that typically takes several years and millions of dollars to complete), but whatever is appropriate make the decision and start that person along the path toward success today.

You may think that you need to be in charge, be the boss, in order to give aspiring leaders development opportunities but that is not necessarily the case. Mentoring takes place at all levels within organizations. Some companies have formal leadership programs, job shadowing, or rotational assignments that you can leverage, but even when you need to go it alone with a little creativity you can be successful. If you are not able to assign work, you can always ask for help. Leverage your network, talk to the folks in charge, and more often than not you'll be pleasantly surprised by how well things turn out.

There are lots of ways to give people who deserve it a shot. Set guiderails where you must, and be a resource when you can, but be cautious not to micromanage the aspiring leader who has been given this opportunity. In order to grow and mature, folks need freedom to figure things out for themselves.

Sensei, Mentor, Teacher, Coach – Little Life Secret:

> Most people grow into challenges. They will step up or down to your expectations. As a college intern Kane was tasked with staffing two restaurants for the Seattle Sheraton, a daunting task for someone with book learning and no practical experience, yet his manager set high expectations, provided resources, and got out of the way. By the end of his tenure, 239 of the 240 people Kane recommended were hired and all performed well on the job. Just because someone is inexperienced does not mean that they should only be allowed to perform entry-level work.

ESPRIT DE CORPS

Four Keys to Group Unanimity

*"Talent wins games, but teamwork
and intelligence wins championships."*
Michael Jordan[4]

We've all heard the phrase, "Coach has lost the locker room." It is a sports axiom meaning that the players no longer buy into their coach's vision. In the locker room, the club house, the inner circle, whatever you want to call it, in the most sacrosanct setting that only those on the team may enter, the coach has no believers. Losing the locker room is a monumentally big deal. Esprit de corps, on the other hand, is the opposite of losing the locker room. Capturing the concept of group unanimity, it is a French phrase that acknowledges the spirit of the corps, the essence of the body, or the mood of the group.

Esprit de corps is about a collection of individuals who truly operate as a team. Together they hold tightly to the common goal that has been set before them, rolling out a new product, building a program, securing a victory, winning a championship. They believe in a collective vision so strongly that they are willing to sacrifice, subordinating their individual desires for the team and the goal.

There are four key ingredients to building esprit de corps:

1. Leadership
2. Will
3. Deference
4. Self-Discipline

The leader must have authority, granted from both above and below, and the group being led must have the will, deference, and self-discipline to carry out their leader's vision. We will explore each of these elements in detail below.

1. Leadership

Power and authority are granted from above and below. For example, General Eisenhower became supreme commander of the allied invasion of Normandy during World War II because both United States President Roosevelt and British Prime Minister Churchill said so. Nevertheless, being in charge is not enough. Eisenhower also held the hearts of most of his immediate subordinates. As the line of command trickled down to lowest private, everyone throughout the military found himself honored to have a battlefield visit with the great Dwight D. Eisenhower, the General and Supreme Allied Commander.

If power is given from above but the troops are not on board, the locker room has been lost. Conversely, if a leader is beloved by his team but his bosses will not listen, he or she cannot be effective. Lose both, and… well let's just say that tends to not end well.

For example, in 2010 Mike Singletary, one the greatest linebackers ever to play in the National Football League, was fired as the coach of the San Francisco Forty-Niners after a 25–17 loss to the St. Louis Rams. Defensive line coach Jim Tomsula was tasked to fill in as interim head coach for the final game of the season against the Arizona Cardinals. While Singletary's team had posted a tumultuous 5–10 record despite being considered the most talent-laden teams in a weak NFC West Conference, the seeds of his demise were planted a couple of years earlier.

In 2008, tight end Vernon Davis committed what Singletary considered a stupid 15-yard penalty during a game that the Forty-Niners were losing. Coach Singletary sent him to the locker room, publicly shaming Davis on national television. Afterward Singletary told the press, "I would rather play with ten people and just get penalized all the way until we've got to do something else, rather than play with eleven when I know that right now that person is not sold out to be a part of this team. It is more about them than it is about the team. Cannot play with them, cannot win with them, cannot coach with them. Can't do it. Can't do it. I want winners. I want people that want to win."

Davis was now, "not a winner." He'd been labeled a sellout and had been treated like a child in front of his peers, flying in the face of one of the hallmarks of good leadership: praising publicly, criticizing privately. Coaches are rarely fired during the season, yet a couple of years later Singletary's rapport with his players had become so bad that the team let him go. The following year Coach Jim Harbaugh, fresh from his 12–1 season and Orange Bowl victory at Stanford University, led the San Francisco Forty-Niners to a 13–3 record with essentially the same personnel who had gone 5–10 under Singletary the previous season.

Without unity of purpose there can be no victory on the field, on the mat, or in hearts of your students or team members. Lose the authority from above, the organization, or ownership, or lose the locker room and you cannot have success. Both are needed for the esprit de corp.

2. Will

The will to do what it takes to achieve, say earn a black belt or win a game, is based on desire. Desire is a powerful word. When a person says they desire something, they are speaking from the heart. The heart is not rational. Emotions that come from the heart such as love or hate are never rational. These emotions make little sense to the intellect, yet they profoundly affect behavior. Another way of saying it is that desires of the heart are non-negotiable.

Anybody who has tried to talk a friend or relative into leaving a bad relationship knows that there is no give-and-take, no productive conversation than can make any difference in matters of the heart. No matter the examples, no matter the proof, the heart will rationalize the situation back to achieve its desire unless overruled by the head, a long and arduous process that does not always succeed. Conversely, when you hear the phrase, "his heart was in it," that is a powerful state of existence.

The will is based in this place, in the heart. If you want something bad enough and that desire comes from the heart, it is rare that you will not find some way to achieve it even when facing significant obstacles. For example, due to a rare birth defect Kyle Maynard was born a congenital amputee, missing his limbs below the elbows and knees. Despite having neither hands nor feet, he refused to let his condition interfere with his goals in life. He learned how to eat, write, and even type 50 words per minute all without relying on the hands he did not have. By the age of nineteen had he played middle school football as a defensive lineman, became a state high school wrestling champion, and established a new world weightlifting record. Mr. Maynard exemplifies the indomitable spirit of someone who refuses to be limited by his disabilities.

In self-defense situations most confrontations end by breaking the adversary's will, not by rendering him or her physically incapable of continuing to fight. Similarly, the team with the most heart in the game often wins despite a disparity of talent. Even in warfare, overcoming another nation's determination to persevere assures victory, not destroying all their resources and murdering all of their people. This is why willpower is so important, vital to virtually any endeavor.

3. Deference

The military in every country across the world teaches obedience, deference not only to authority figures but also to the goals and objectives of the organization. Obedience must be possessed by the soldier, team, or the employee, or chaos reigns when orders are not carried out. The challenge is that obedience is always best given rather than demanded. Respect is vital, without it the team will only follow you as far as they must to satisfy your expectations. A soldier's oath, a pledge of allegiance, or a corporate code of conduct, these are all examples of deference.

Many students only attend public schools in the United States because it is mandated by law. They have to be at school, but they don't have to actively participate. Administrators and teachers recognize this fact and allow for self-segregation. Some students, those who truly want to learn and have the ability to handle the materials, find themselves in Advanced Placement or honors classes, while others choose to not participate in such programs. As incongruent as it may sound at first blush, a student must first have the will to be obedient to the vision the education system is espousing before he or she can learn anything.

Obedience isn't blind, however. Soldiers are bound to follow lawful orders, not their commander's every whim (in volunteer armies at least). Subordinates should have leeway to exercise discretion, ingenuity, and self-direction so long as they are working toward a common goal. They defer to the leader's vision, embracing his or her leadership due to respect and trust. A quarterback may call an audible during a football game, for example, but he is still using his coach's playbook.

Deference is not subservience, but it does require subordinating one's ambitions to further the organization's cause. That is much easier for most people to do when they believe that in making the team or organization successful their individual goals will be accomplished along the way.

4. Self-Discipline

Anyone who has tried to lose weight knows how hard it can be to stick to a plan, even when you know it's the right thing to do. It's not just a matter of willpower, but also of self-discipline. Desire comes from the heart, while discipline comes from the head. The combination of the two can lead you to great things. Self-discipline manifests in time management, diligence, and other factors necessary to stay on track and accomplish your goals.

For example, Susan Butcher was one of Alaska's most famous athletes. Competing in a traditionally male-dominated sport, she won the world's longest sled dog race, the Iditarod, a historic four times. Braving grueling conditions such as subzero temperatures, blinding snowstorms, treacherous ice, dangerous wildlife, and sleep deprivation to mush 1,152 miles from Anchorage to Nome, she made the trek 17 times during her racing career.

In 1985 she was forced to defend herself and her dog team from an attacking bull moose, an approximately 1,200 pound beast, using only her ice axe and parka. The moose stomped two of her dogs to death and injured 13 more before another musher came along and shot it. Butcher, who withdrew after the loss of her dog team, was leading the race at the time. Had that incident not occurred she very well may have won five Iditarod races, tying an all-time record. While she ultimately lost her struggle with leukemia in 2006, Butcher demonstrated the same bravery and grit in battling her illness that she did competing in the Iditarod.

You probably don't have to struggle against nature's fury while competing against other dog teams, but getting up early to hit the weight room before school, polishing your skills, watching game film, and the like all are parts of focused self-discipline that makes you a better athlete and more effective team member. Likewise in business, continuing education credits, certification tests, symposiums and the like are all aspects of keeping your mind sharp and your skills fresh. It takes concerted effort to fit such things into an already hectic schedule, demonstrating that in all endeavors, self-discipline is necessary for high achievement.

Team Dynamics

> *"I was fortunate to be a captain of both my high school and college football teams when I was growing up. On my high school football team we had a 2–7 record. My college football team went 9–0. Each team had great players, yet there was a major difference in the results. The difference was the 9–0 team put the team goals ahead of individual goals. The most important part to the 9–0 team was the success of the team. We knew that if we did that, the individual goals would come. At times we are operating like a 2–7 team where individual goals are more important today. How do we consistently operate like the 9–0 team instead of like the 2–7 team?"* – Dave Schmidt[5]

New teams virtually never mesh instantly, even when comprised of seasoned professionals. They tend to go through a phased cycle, something that psychologist Bruce Tuckman first postulated in 1965 as (1) forming, (2) storming, (3) norming, and (4) performing. This process not only works for a new team, but also for existing ones where new members are introduced into the mix. Many folks add a fifth stage, "mourning," to Tuckman's list to include the point where a team is disbanded at the end of a project or where a significant change in membership takes place such as at the end of a college basketball season when key players graduate.

The five phases of teaming work as follows:

1. **Forming**: members are brought together and tasked with an assignment to accomplish. The forming stage is usually fairly short in duration, but includes the process of members getting to know each other and figuring out who is responsible for what aspect of the project. In business a team charter document tends to be commonplace to help expedite this process. On sports teams it can include an orientation where players are assigned to positions.
2. **Storming**: members' emotions often come into play as they clarify the team's goals and objectives, jockey for position within the roles, and collectively reach commitment about what will be done. In business an RAA (Responsibility, Accountability, and Authority) document tends to be commonplace to expedite this process. On sports teams it can include competitions that stratify rankings within each position (such as starters, second string players, etc.). This is the time period when the team leader or coach's conflict resolution skills must shine as the chances of disagreement amongst team members are high and it is vital that disputes do not linger or metastasize into longstanding resentments.
3. **Norming**: once team members have gotten to know each other better and feel comfortable with their assignments, they can formulate how best to work together to reach the superiorordinate goal. There is often a prolonged overlap between storming and norming phases. As new

challenges arise, the team may lapse back into typical storming stage behavior such as blaming each other for difficulties, but in most cases proactive leadership causes this behavior to die out over time.
4. **Performing**: the group culture is strong enough that all individuals function effectively as a team, even when challenges or interpersonal conflicts arise. For high performance teams, a light touch is necessary to assure that things remain on track, but oftentimes the team leader (e.g., head coach) can begin to delegate more and more of the responsibility to key members (e.g., position coaches or coordinators), affording opportunities for others to learn and grow.
5. **Mourning**: most teams disband at some point due to successful completion of the project, culmination of the deployment, organizational realignment, reassignment of priorities, end of the season, or whatever. It is usually advisable to hold a ceremony of some type for closure such as an awards banquet to assure that the experience ends on a high note. Even in a losing season, certain players shine and should be recognized for doing so (see Chapter 17, Recognizing Effort for more information).

A challenge of the storming and norming phases, particularly the latter, is the need for members to establish a hierarchy and cement their positions within the team. This stage is where some form of hazing is commonplace since team members need to viscerally know that they can count on each other when the proverbial feces hits the oscillating blades. This is particularly important for tactical operators and sports teams, but can also be necessary in high stress, competitive business settings as well.

Pay close attention to how this unfolds. There are good ways, bad ways, and politically acceptable ways for team members to understand each other's capabilities and develop mutual respect. If channeled properly this can be a good thing. For example, some professional sports teams require their rookie players to perform a skit, pay for an end of training camp celebration, or put on a talent show. Clearly there is potential for these types of activities to become embarrassing, but in a good natured way. If undirected, however, the norming phase may spark a headline-generating hazing incident that damages the organization's reputation and becomes a career-killer for everyone involved.

For example, it's hard to imagine anyone bullying a 300-pound NFL lineman, save perhaps for another 300-pound lineman, but that is apparently what took place between Miami Dolphins players Richie Incognito and Jonathan Martin. In what allegedly began as a series of hazing incidents that spiraled out of control, news reports state that among other things Incognito sent racist, threatening text messages to his teammate Martin who left the team when he felt he could no longer take the abuse. Incognito was subsequently suspended by Dolphins Head Coach Joe Philbin.

The HBO series *Hard Knocks* which chronicled the Dolphins' training camp in 2012 showed several hazing incidents, but Coach Philbin who never watched the program claimed he was unaware of the situation making some wonder about his control over the team. Nevertheless he launched an investigation, stating in a press conference, "If the review shows that this is not a safe atmosphere, I will take whatever measures are necessary to ensure that it is. I have that obligation to the players that I coach on a daily basis and I will do that."

For the first six games of the year before Martin left the team over the alleged bullying, he and Incognito were the two players assigned to protect quarterback Ryan Tannehill's blind side. Their troubled relationship may help explain why Tannehill was sacked an NFL-high 35 times. The hazing allegations also sparked comments and bad press across the league, with players and coaches wondering why no one intervened. "You would hope if stuff was getting out of hand there were guys in the locker room who would step up and maybe nip it in the bud before it got out of control," Tennessee Titans cornerback Jason McCourty told the press.

To compound the Dolphins' troubles, they were lampooned by Spirit Airlines when the company released an advertisement, "Don't be bullied by high fares. Fly incognito out of Florida, or any place for that matter." The words not only appeared in Miami's team colors but the photo accompanying it also showed a guy in a business suit wearing a white helmet with aqua and orange stripes.

As the controversy developed many Dolphins' players including Tannehill defended Philbin, his staff, Incognito, and their teammates. Current and former players from other teams weighed in as well. And the NFL launched an investigation. Fingers were pointed, accusations were made, and the reputations of the Miami Dolphins coaching staff and players were diminished in the process.

Sensei, Mentor, Teacher, Coach Tip:

> When you dive down deep into the esprit de corps, it is like looking at an atom. If all the parts are in place—say two hydrogen atoms and one oxygen atom (H_2O)—then you get the desired output, which in this example is water. Change the equation to one hydrogen atom and one oxygen atom and the molecule becomes unbalanced. It will seek stability by acquiring another hydrogen atom. Similarly, people who lack one of the three essential elements, will, deference, or self-discipline, are unstable. It is difficult to find balance when one of the three legs of the stool is lacking. While self-directed people will find this missing element on their own, others need to have it shown to them. The ability to find the gap, explain the need, and show others the way can make you a great leader.

Action:

Pay close attention to your team, assuring that all four elements of esprit de corps are in place. Leadership is your responsibility, whereas will, deference, and self-discipline must come from your crew. Where any element is lacking changes may be required. Assure that you have the right charter and governance, that your oversight is appropriate for both the people and the mission, and that you have surrounded yourself with the right personnel for success.

As Lou Holtz, the famous Notre Dame Football coach once said, "Not everybody can be first team, but you can always put the team first."

No matter what the makeup of your group it is vital to monitor the dynamics in play throughout all five stages of the team lifecycle, being especially cautious during the storming and norming phases. Keeping your organization's culture and expectations in mind, use a methodical approach to team-building such as a leadership retreat, ropes course, Outward Bound experience, paintball game, or the like to channel the energy in a positive direction. The activity itself is far less important than the structure it provides.

Sensei, Mentor, Teacher, Coach – Little Life Secret:

> Most leaders understand that it is their responsibility to support their team members' growth and development. Oftentimes, however, bosses are reluctant to let their best people move on to other opportunities, finding them "too important" to let go, despite the obvious morale implications of such actions. That is a "lose-lose" proposition if ever there was one. Instead, flip things around to the other direction. One of the best ways to become promotable is to have your own replacement trained and ready to fill in straight away. It tends to lighten the workload too.

3

PROBLEMS ARE NORMAL

Six Ways to Instantly Improve Problem Solving

"Problems are normal; treat them that way."
Al Davis[6]

During his storied career Al Davis, owner of the NFL's Oakland Raiders, was a head coach, general manager, and league commissioner. He helped form both the American Football League and the National Football League. His Oakland Raiders have won the Super Bowl three times. No small achievements.

Successful people like Davis do not assume that all is going to go according to plan. That means that they put good people in place and trust their team to make good choices, yet they also know people are human and things can go sideways if not monitored. Monitoring is not micromanaging. Leaders who get their plans executed are people who pay attention to detail, yet do not meddle. Not only do they strike this delicate balance, they also realize that problems are normal and deal with them accordingly.

This realization that problems are normal is not an acceptance, a willingness to let things go off course; it is simply a fact. The natural state of the world is not convergence, everything coming together. It is about entropy, the degradation of systems. That does not mean that there is nothing you can do about it, of course, but it does require investing time and energy to keep things on track. As a leader you not only have to deal with it, but you have to do so strategically. There is simply not enough time in the day to accomplish everything so you decide how and where you are going to put your energy to make the most impact at any given time.

Every system, be it a sports team, a business, a college, or a martial arts school, has to be fed energy. This energy is needed to stave off the ever-present entropy. As the leader you are often the primary feeder and director of the energy necessary to stave off problems.

Problems can fall into two basic groups: external and internal. External problems are obstacles that come from outside of a system, in this case outside your body. These issues in fact belong to your student, your athlete, your employee, but oftentimes you need to deal with them nevertheless. They can be horribly disruptive as any home, life, or work imbalance can retard learning or athletic performance.

Some issues are minor bumps in the road where you can afford to let things play out without expending much if any energy, while others can be much more severe. For example, there are few things more disruptive than relationship issues. Getting dumped by a longtime girlfriend or boyfriend is tough enough, but a divorce can be emotionally catastrophic for many people. Whether one is involved directly or tangentially (as a child, relative, boss, subordinate, or coworker), the atomic blast of divorce is emotionally devastating and is as selective as radioactive fallout in who it affects.

Students struggling with grades, failing tests, or not getting into the university that they thought was essential to their future can result in anything from a shoulder shrug to a complete breakdown of their self-esteem. Similarly, if work is not going well, the company is on the bubble as to whether or not it is going to remain in business next week, it has become evident that a person's job is going to be outsourced, management restructuring is in play, or your team member knows he or she about to be replaced, there can be a significant impact. This is about home and heart, the ability to provide for one's self and family. Self-worth is an essential aspect of any high-performing individual.

All of these external problems are ones that are difficult to manage from a distance. It is generally inadvisable to become directly involved unless you are a counselor, therapist, priest, or the like. However, as a leader you can and should provide empathy, stability, and consistency of environment and expectations which will hearten those facing any of these external problems.

One of the most effective leadership traits of high-performing managers is consistency, as subordinates know what is expected and how to succeed. It can create real comfort during challenging times. Consistency is built around repetition, a known experience where it does not feel quite so much like the earth is constantly moving underneath the overstressed individual. That is something you can do whether you are the boss, the coworker, or a friend. Even subordinates can do it to some degree, lightening the workload, providing emotional support, and giving their manager one less thing to worry about.

Internal problems are the ones that you experience within yourself. We will be going into more depth in regard to those issues in the next chapter where we discuss flawed thinking, so we will stick to dealing with external problems here. When somebody comes to you with a problem, there are six essential elements you need in order to successfully assist them. These include (1) Setting a time limit, (2) Being a reporter, (3) Leveraging the angels of the angles for good communication, (4) Expressing empathy, (5) Understanding their agenda, and (6) Using thoughtful speech.

1. Set a time limit

How big is your organization? Do you have a hundred players, seventy five employees, thirty students? A mere twenty minutes apiece times ten people and you've taken up nearly half your day without doing anything other than listening to problems. No matter how deeply you care, no matter how empathetic you are, no matter how much time you have available, it will never be enough if you do not set limits.

> *"Coach, I'm having a problem in algebra and I need to talk to you about it."*

> *"I have five minutes before the next class starts. Is that sufficient, or do we need more time? I have office hours on Thursday…"*

Consider the dialogue above. What has happened with this example is that the student understands that you are willing to deal with the problem. If you are able to handle it immediately you will, but you are time-constrained. Limited time forces people to get to the point and not wallow in the emotion that the issue may have around it. They believe that you have some path to resolution for their problem and you are willing to share it and give them the time. However you are limiting it, making it obvious in polite fashion that they need to get to the point so that you can assist them.

Being available is important. Teachers set up office hours, managers schedule "1:1s;" every successful leader finds some way to be visible and available for their team. Part of empathy is assuring that your folks know that you will be there for them when they need you. That is good. In certain instances you need to drop everything and listen to a team member's problem. But, make sure that you manage your time effectively or you will never get anything else done.

2. Be a reporter

Good reporters need to understand facts, the 5 Ws and an H—Who, What, Where, When, Why, and How. These are the basic elements necessary to figure out what has occurred and present the evidence in a clear, informative manner. If a person comes to you with an issue, you need to understand what is going on before you can offer up meaningful advice. Being clear on these five questions will keep you from jumping to conclusions.

We are not suggesting that you approach this as an interrogator, however. We are simply saying that sometimes it is difficult for people under emotional duress to effectively communicate the five elements that are needed to make a good decision. It is your job to make sure that you can get that information from them so that you can cut to the meat of the problem. If you may find yourself looking at an incomplete story it is possible that some of the information is being withheld for a reason; possibly it is due to embarrassment or perhaps the person does not feel it serves their purpose, supports the picture that they are trying to paint.

Be careful about making determinations without relevant facts and data. This does not mean waiting until you know absolutely everything. Due to the speed of modern business, many decisions need to be made with at best 80 percent of the relevant information, yet that is sufficient to make reasoned choices in most instances. That is what you are aiming for as well, enough data to provide a beneficial response. There is almost never a perfect answer.

Keep in mind that oftentimes the person bringing you the problem also has an answer in mind and is looking for validation, a proverbial shoulder to cry on, or a way to vent, so be sure to understand both the open and hidden messages before jumping to a solution that may or may not actually be wanted. This takes active listening.

Active listening is a skill widely taught to business leaders, educators, and law enforcement officers because it is so effective. It helps with everything from getting along with your significant other to dealing with violent criminals. There is no downside to this skill, yet most people do not use it, in part because they spend more time thinking about how they will respond than they do paying attention to what the other person is actually saying. In most conversations, person A says something and halfway through the sentence person B has decided what is about to be said, has formulated a reply, and is mentally rehearsing his or her lines. From that point on, person B is not listening. Real communication has already stopped.

Communication is deeper and more useful if both people are fully engaged. The basics of active listening include:

- **Paying attention**: look at the person talking. Let them see you looking at them. Do not glance at the clock or your watch. Do not start typing on your keyboard, texting on your smartphone, or looking out the window. Shut down your own mind and listen. Listen. Listen all the way through. Then pause and think about it. A pause before answering can also work as a "pattern interrupt." Because you are obviously thinking and listening, the other person must slow down to figure out what is going on. That forces

them to stop counting on their own mental scripts and become fully engaged as well.
- **Asking open-ended questions**: remember that this is about gathering the 5 Ws and an H. You want to ask questions that cannot be answered with one word. "Did you get into an argument with Sally?" is closed. "What happened when you and Sally interacted early today?" is open. The latter encourages a story. You don't just learn from the narrative of events, you also learn about the other person by what he or she emphasizes or leaves out, what makes them excited or subdued.
- **Concentrate on emotion and demeanor**: when the words say one thing and the emotion says another, bet on emotion for true motive (we talk about this more in Chapter 14). It can also be a clue when you paraphrase. For that matter, pay attention to your own emotions, not just to those of the person communicating with you. Sometimes there are hints, subtleties your subconscious noticed that have not yet made it to your conscious brain. If you find yourself getting agitated, angry, or anxious pause for a moment and figure out why. It can be illuminating.
- **Use paraphrasing to demonstrate understanding**: double-check your understanding by repeating back the other person's key points in your own words. "Let me see if I got this right..." It is good to clear up any miscommunication early. This may also be the time to point out body language or incongruities that make you doubt the other person's words where appropriate. You can get huge amounts of information when people try to clarify, especially when they are trying to explain away obvious emotion while struggling to seem calm.

3. **Leverage the angels of the angles for good communication**

There's an old kindergarten song that is sung by almost every child at one time or another. The little song is easy to remember because the title of it is *Head, Shoulders, Knees, and Toes*. While singing, each kindergartner touches the appropriate part of their body—head, shoulders, knees, and toes—doing a nice little warm-up exercise to begin their day. This song is not just for kids, however; it is a key to body language that you can use to open the lines of communication with whomever you are talking with.

- **Head**: head position communicates an enormous amount of information. Turned slightly sideways looking with one eye denotes suspicion. Holding your chin too high indicates a position of superiority making it difficult for somebody in a subordinate position to communicate. Looking down over the top of your glasses… that equals condescension. The best head technique to get more information out of another person is a simple nod, up and down for yes. Yes I hear you, yes I understand you, and yes that makes sense. There are more things that can go wrong than can go right with head position; we suggest this simple technique to avoid them.
- **Shoulders**: proxemics comes into play here. Standing directly in front of someone who is not a close friend or family member with your shoulders squared to them will result in a lizard-brain response. What we mean by lizard brain is that they will immediately dive into "fight, flight, or freeze" mode. It is difficult for a person to engage the cognitive aspects of their upper brain when their hindbrain is telling them that it is fight-or-flight time. To avoid this reaction, stand like people do at bars or other social events, with the shoulders at an angle. Another guideline is to imagine a laser beam emitting from your bellybutton. Your laser beam should not align with the other person's but rather these two laser beams should cross out in space in front of you. To place your shoulders squarely is a technique used by military drill instructors; it does have a place and you may choose to use it for dominant positioning or to reinforce hierarchical authority when communicating simple commands, but for deep communication it is the wrong tactic. Don't overuse it.
- **Knees and toes**: pointing the foot in the direction of what you are trying to explain is a subtle technique that allows for you to focus the other person's attention toward

the subject at hand. For instance, a coach discussing a defensive back's behavior to a wide receiver can point his toe in the direction of the occurrence setting attention to that moment. It allows them to discuss something that happened in the past in very real terms by focusing the athlete's mind on exactly what occurred. The student can replay the moment, understanding the complexity of what took place with little interference from the lizard brain.

4. Express empathy

"I understand."

The simple phrase "I understand" is a great opener once you have established the 5 Ws and an H. We also suggest adding the aforementioned head nod and then repeat the problem back to the person you are speaking with in your own words. Oftentimes, sharing a personal experience that helps demonstrate the fact that you truly do understand. However, being a one-upper is counterproductive. In other words, sharing a problem that you had that was much grander than the other person's and telling them how you overcame it can unintentionally make them feel stupid for bringing their issue up in the first place. Remember that the conversation is about *them*, not you, and act accordingly. And, be sure that the speaker is actually looking for a solution before offering one.

When someone brings you a problem they are not interested in your story, they are interested in your empathy. For example, if a student says that he is having trouble in a math class, the appropriate response might be that yes head nod, followed by the simple phrase, "I understand." And to say something to the effect of, "You're not the only one who has difficulty with the class. This Advanced Placement program is a college class taught at the high school level, so it's designed to be tough." And then to come forward with a potential solution such as, "What we've done in the past with some students is to have a teacher's assistant to help them with their studies. If you think that would help I can set it up for you. It will add to your homework load, but it should help you improve your grades. Does that sound like that's something you would be willing to do?"

The cool thing about empathy is that most decent people already have it in spades, though most don't express it naturally. That's where active listening comes in, it simultaneously assures that you understand the situation and are able to make the other person feel like you care enough to help them find a way to resolve it.

5. Understand their agenda

When somebody comes forward with a problem you need to find their agenda. There are really only two choices, a very simple decision tree with two branches. The first branch is to escape responsibility, whereas the second branch is to grow into the responsibility. Your job as a mentor, teacher, or coach is to find out which one of these two paths the person is trying to exercise and deal with it accordingly.

While it may seem that a person should always grow into the responsibility that is not always practicable, particularly when timeframes are short. You've probably heard the term "upward delegation." More often than not it's an attempt to dodge responsibility, but sometimes it is appropriate. You are the leader for a reason. You have access to knowledge, skills, or resources that others do not. That does not necessarily mean that you should automatically take on their problem and make it your problem, however.

Leaders help break down roadblocks, acquire resources, and resolve problems, but they cannot and should not do everything themselves. Good leaders stick to what they can control or influence. Lay out the best path to resolution that you can see, but resist the temptation to boil the proverbial ocean for things that are beyond your scope of responsibility.

6. Use thoughtful speech

When you are approached with a problem you will often need to slow down the rate at which you speak. Slow speech with pauses demonstrates thoughtfulness and care. It is a natural output of active listening. Further, slowing things down (within reason) tends to make the communication special.

Look to the entertainment industry by way of example. When they want to make something seem special, say an action scene or a moment of great importance in a film, they slow things down—cinematography, speech, or action. An example found in virtually all action movies is a massive, slow motion explosion. So, take your lead from people who make trillions of dollars by controlling audience emotions and entertaining people. By simply slowing down your rate of speech and adding thoughtful pauses you will come across as more engaged, involved, and thoughtful.

One simple technique for doing this is to count to three before responding to the other person. You may have already constructed your mental response, but the pause demonstrates thoughtfulness, that their issue has real meaning to you. Once you have that connection you can begin successful communication. Further, slowing things down when you can allows for deeper thought. If you want to make something special follow the Hollywood trick of slowing the moment down; it facilitates greater observation as well.

The way other people read your emotion and intent is through the rate, tone, pitch and volume of your voice. Rate and volume are indicators of intensity, whereas tone and pitch indicate the quality of emotion. The more excited someone is, whether anger or fear or even love, the louder they tend to be. And the faster they talk. This is part of why speaking slowly can denote wisdom. Don't overdo it though. Speaking too slowly can be perceived as having a lack of wit. Acceptable rates tend to vary regionally. Unless you're communicating with someone from another country or geography you should have a reasonable idea of the correct pacing.

Tone can be difficult to define in a meaningful way, but take the example of a guitar and piano both playing the same note (pitch) at the same volume. They still sound different. That difference is the tone. In this manner, you have probably experienced the fact that anger, fear, and frustration all sound viscerally different even though you'd likely have a difficult time explaining exactly why.

By paying attention to the rate, tone, pitch and volume of the speaker's voice and controlling your own you will have a better chance of communicating effectively. You may be caught up in the emotion, but by thoughtfully slowing your speech and exercising active-listening you will have a better chance of understanding and resolving issues that are brought to you for solutions.

Sensei, Mentor, Teacher, Coach Tip:

> Problems are problems. They are normal and expected, so much so that if everything went according to plan you would probably have nothing to do. Embrace these challenges as opportunities to make things better for yourself and your team.

Action:

No matter how busy you are it is vital to make yourself available for your team. Open door policies are fine, but events of the day tend to overwhelm if you aren't proactive about setting aside time. Schedule recurring one-on-one meetings, face-to-face whenever possible, that give those around you a chance to talk on a weekly or bi-weekly basis. They do not have to be long, ten to fifteen minutes in duration works fine in many cases, but whatever the amount you are able to allot be sure to give your full attention to the person you are conversing with. The agenda should be up to the team member, consider it their time not yours. If, on any given week, it turns out that there's nothing to discuss you can always cancel, though the optics are better if you do so only at the team members' request.

When somebody comes to you with a problem, make sure that they are actually asking for help. If so, use the problem solving structure to set a time limit, be a reporter, utilize the right body language for good communication, express empathy, understand their agenda, and employ thoughtful speech. In this fashion you can come up with well-reasoned solutions while simultaneously building rapport with your team. We discuss ways to think beyond the obvious and form creative solutions in more depth in Chapter 5.

Sensei, Mentor, Teacher, Coach – Little Life Secret:

> People generally prefer to avoid conflict, so it takes guts for someone to come to you with a problem, particularly when they think you might be the cause of their dilemma. While it is easy to be offended, do your best not to take such things personally. You are acting on behalf of your organization; to the employee you are the company, to the player you are the team, so keep your responses professional. It is easier to do so when you consider that a hallmark of good leadership is the fact that your team member found you approachable enough to express their concern in the first place.

4

FLAWED THINKING

Fifteen Negative Attitudes to Banish from Your Brain

"It's fine to celebrate success but it is more important to heed the lessons of failure."
Bill Gates[7]

Kane has interviewed and hired hundreds of people. When he was first assigned that responsibility a quarter century ago, he was required to take a course on rater errors. The curriculum covered concepts you would probably recognize such as the first impression bias and the "similar to me" effect which, though innovative at the time, made intuitive sense to attendees. The company simultaneously tracked employee performance, helping to validate effectiveness of managers in vetting and hiring qualified personnel. While no class can categorically assure objective, unbiased results, this data demonstrated that simply pointing out natural tendencies helped well-intentioned folks become more aware of their predispositions and keep natural biases from unduly influencing their decisions.

Our goal in this section is similar to that rater errors class, helping you become aware of preconceived notions that may distort your thinking in unproductive ways so that you can minimize if not eliminate their impact. Distorted thinking tends to bring negative thoughts to the forefront, inhibiting performance and achievement. Left unaddressed it can become a self-fulfilling prophecy which is detrimental for you or any member of your team who gets caught up in this behavior.

The following fifteen types of distorted thinking are adapted from the work of psychologists McKay, Davis, and Fanning. The original concept was published in 1981 in their book *Thoughts & Feelings*. It is a great resource that can help address anxiety, frustration, and many other negative emotions using cognitive therapy techniques.

The fifteen distortions include (1) Filtering, (2) Polarized thinking, (3) Overgeneralization, (4) Mindreading, (5) Catastrophizing, (6) Personalization, (7) External control, (8) Internal control, (9) Fairness, (10) Blaming, (11) Must, (12) Emotional reasoning, (13) Resisting change, (14) Being right, and (15) Heaven's reward. We will briefly explain each distortion, provide our recommendations for overcoming it, and then give you some "homework," a task of the week.

If you accept our challenge and tackle these tasks over the next fifteen weeks you will notice a marked change in your thinking. Like rater error interview training it will not make you a different person, but it will make you keenly aware of what you may have been unconsciously doing and kick-start a change in your perception.

1. Filtering

> *"Exaggeration is truth that has lost its temper."*
> Khalil Gibran[8]

Filtering is when you take details and magnify them to the extreme, distorting actual events. A single element is picked out and the whole event becomes colored by this facet. Much like spending a wonderful evening on a date only to focus on the parking ticket you received while you were dining, when you pull negative things out of context, isolated from all the good experiences around you, you make them larger and more awful than they truly are. This can result in biased or prejudicial thinking when focused externally on others, or in becoming sad or depressed if focused internally on yourself.

An example of this is often found in business. For instance, a handful of customers or students might be habitually late with their payments. The ongoing behavior of two or three bad apples is projected onto all of the clients when, in fact, 98% are on time. This 2% darkens your attitude with everyone, filtering and contaminating your relationships with the majority.

Flawed Thinking

We recommend:

Strive to look at things holistically. When a negative event takes place put it into context. For example, Kane recently forgot to lock his truck. Someone rifled through the contents and stole all the change out of his ashtray (it's an old truck). While he was upset at losing a few bucks, he felt fortunate that the vehicle was undamaged and took it as a lesson to keep things secured rather than a statement on the inherent untrustworthiness of humanity. A vandalized vehicle, stolen radio, slashed tire, or the like would have been a much bigger inconvenience, harder to replace than a few bucks in pocket change.

Task of the week:

For the next week avoid using (and in fact seek out and destroy from your vocabulary) extreme words such as, "always," "never," "every time," and "all the time." These words can oftentimes be construed as accusatory. For example, "You always do XY&Z." We've all said that, yet we also know that nobody always does something, every time, all the time. For next seven days cut all accusatory words and phrases from your communication.

2. **Polarized thinking**

> *"Morals are private. Decency is public."*
> Rita Mae Brown[9]

Black and white thinking is a method of building fences around acceptable and unacceptable behavior, making all issues cut and dried. There is no shade of grey, no context, and no exceptions. For example, in 1928 baseball great Ty Cobb went into the stands and beat a fan named Claude Lueker unconscious because the guy had hurled insults about Cobb's mother. Cobb firmly believed that his honor and, more importantly, his mother's honor had been insulted. In Cobb's black and white worldview, he had no choice but to lay a beat down on the other guy (who happened to be disabled, confined to a wheelchair, and missing several fingers from an industrial accident). Polarized thinking has no room for context. Would Cobb have beat a five-year old senseless for hurling insults about his mother? Well, perhaps he might have, but as a leader you understand that correcting a child requires different behavior than coaching an adult. The same thing applies to much in life. Few issues have no room for context.

We recommend:

Take a hard look at your moral code. In much of life shades of grey are appropriate. Take murder for example. Killing someone is clearly frowned upon by modern society, but as horrendous as homicide is there is still an exception made in cases of legitimate self-defense. Are you drawing lines in the right places?

Task of the Week:

Look for a salacious news article, something that is big, controversial, and well covered such as a prominent murder trial (e.g., Arias, Simpson, or Zimmerman) and dig deeper, finding at least four divergent different sources for analysis. If, for example, you're in the United States, search for perspectives from CNN, Fox, *The New York Times*, and *The Washington Post*. Then, find additional coverage from outside the country; say the *Financial Times of London* or *Al Jazeera*. Examine the biases of those reporting and try to articulate them. Compare and contrast these perspectives with your own view. It's a lot of work but should prove illuminating.

3. Overgeneralization

> *"On the whole human beings want to be good, but not too good, and not quite all the time."*
> George Orwell[10]

Overgeneralization has been an issue for quite some time, but with today's social and electronic media it seems to be a growing problem. Small aspects of a person's actions or personality are extrapolated out to be an all-encompassing statement of their being. Even "positive" overgeneralizations can be problematic. For example, stereotypes like "all Asians are good at math" downplay hard work of the individual. People are much more complex than overgeneralization allows.

Our judicial system has a built-in acknowledgment of the power of overgeneralization. Past behaviors tend to predict future behaviors, yet lapses in judgment or youthful indiscretions do not necessarily imply that a person is fundamentally flawed. By using probation and education we believe that offenders can be rehabilitated. We even go so far as to, in some instances, have youthful crimes expunged from a person's record once they reach adulthood.

Overgeneralizing about yourself, particularly when looking at your faults, can have an insidious impact upon your self-esteem. Overgeneralizing about others can lead to snap-judgments, relationship problems, prejudice, or even discrimination.

We recommend:

Similar to filtering, overgeneralization can get you into trouble. Judge yourself and others based on their individual actions and accomplishments, weighing the good and the bad in an attempt to reach a holistic appraisal. There is a difference between who you are and what you do. Even good people make mistakes. Focus on the behaviors.

Easier said than done, right? Sometimes the best way to break through emotion is to write things down. The simple act of writing helps you focus on evidence and organize your thoughts. Shrewd observation backed up by facts and data can lead you to the truth. Consider pertinent elements such as specific behaviors that you have observed, how people are progressing against their goals, and accomplishments that can be enumerated in an empirical way.

Task of the week:

If you listen to political ads you have undoubtedly heard that all Republicans want to starve children to death and that all Democrats want to take everything you earn and redistribute it to someone more deserving than you. These statements are examples of extreme overgeneralizations that have no place in leadership.

What if instead of political parties we switched it around to race, gender, sexual orientation, or religion? For example, what if we told you that all white people want to starve children to death and all black people want to steal everything you earn. Makes you shiver just reading that doesn't it? Overgeneralizations about skin color are repugnant, disgusting, and racist, yet the same qualities based on a person's political affiliation are generally considered acceptable. They should not be.

This week you must look to a group that you do not identify with and learn something about them. You do not need to make this a formal research project; you can do it via the web, a documentary, or whatever you like… just find a reputable source. By the end of the week you should be able list three attributes that you find admirable about this group. Do the same thing for a group you already find admirable and identify three attributes that you find offensive about them.

For instance the Spartans are often pointed to as one of the greatest warrior societies in history. We speak glowingly about the famous battle of Thermopylae in 480 BC, an event immortalized in books and film, where 300 Spartan warriors gallantly died holding off the mighty Persian army that outnumbered them nearly 850 to 1. But Spartans also practiced infanticide, killing the less-than-desirable children via exposure, a slow, cruel death for a defenseless newborn. Another example is that you might think that government-provided healthcare is a great thing, which is exactly what Hitler said when he brought socialized medicine to post World War I Germany.

Overgeneralization is a dangerous game for a true leader.

4. Mindreading

> *"It is the mark of an educated mind to be able to entertain a thought without accepting it."*
> Aristotle[11]

You know what a strawberry tastes like, but do you know what a strawberry tastes like to your friend? You probably think that you know, but you don't. No one can. Projecting what others are thinking, their feelings toward you, or assuming that they think the same way about an issue that you do is, well, mindreading. It is not a safe method of operation as a coach, teacher, or mentor. Mindreading allows us to avoid finding out what others really think. It is lazy and unproductive, and oftentimes leads to unnecessary confrontation.

We recommend:

This is one of those cases where an ounce of prevention really is worth a pound of cure. If you suspect that something is not correct, it probably isn't going well. Figure out the problem. Don't mind-read; ask the tough questions. If the issue is allowed to grow it only becomes more difficult, more unwieldy to deal with. As a leader it is your job to know the truth.

Task of the week:

This week you are alien to the planet. You are to assume little. Investigation and precision are the tone of the week, to exercise your inquiry muscle and your clarity bones. You are to ask the questions such as, "Tell me more about that" or "Please restate that another way." "Say that again" is not to be used, however, because people will simply repeat themselves rather than bringing new concepts or explanations to the idea.

We often speak in brief terms and shorten ideas into metaphors or analogies. It is a form of shorthand that speaks to the picture-driven mind, particularly for visual learners. This can be an effective form of communication but it is often based on common cultural experience and is tempered by situations you are personally familiar with. For example, someone might be seeking your counsel on dealing with his difficult child. If he had an abusive, alcoholic parent then asking, "What would any father do in this situation?" may not achieve the desired results. There is no common context to draw from.

We've all heard the joke, "'Assume makes an Ass out of U and Me." Crude, but true. Probing for understanding, asking for more, and actively listening (which we discussed in Chapter 3) can set up a far more meaningful conversation. That's your job this week.

5. Catastrophizing

> "All cartoon characters and fables must be exaggeration, caricatures. It is the very nature of fantasy and fable."
> Walt Disney[12]

Catastrophizing is a youthful emotion, a practice of declaring that, "The whole world hates me!" What parent or schoolteacher has not seen catastrophizing in all its adolescent glory? However, the phenomenon is not limited to youth. Catastrophizing regularly manifests from the mouths of virtually every newscaster, politician, and pundit.

Take a sportscast, for example. Every moment of the game, whatever game you happen to be watching, is emotionally charged. If you're a soccer fan, how many times have you heard, "Gooooooooooaaaaaaaaaaal!!!" shouted by the announcer? According to the broadcasters the contest is without any shadow of a doubt racing toward some horrific conclusion for the home team, visitors, or whoever happens to be behind at the time. We all know that more often than not dire predictions are not true, but the tension helps keeps fans riveted to their television screen.

Without some manufactured catastrophe looming politicians, pundits, and news people would have trouble keeping their jobs. Certainly their importance would be reduced. That's why proverbial dirty laundry is front page news. For instance, Kane's parents were vacationing at Yellowstone National Park in 1988 when the infamous forest fire broke out. It was a significant event, but comparing the pictures they brought back against the ones shown on the news made it clear that CNN took great care with their camera angles to show as much devastation as possible. In the news videos the entire place was on fire, whereas in the home movies it was a much smaller swath of land that was ablaze.

If you expect calamity, chances are good that you will find it, yet most times it is either not real or dramatically less impactful than you have been led to believe. The challenge is that you cannot

Flawed Thinking

mitigate a problem that feels so enormous it's unsolvable. You need to get your head in the right place to see it for what it truly is first.

We Recommend:

Whether it stems from your own imagination run wild or you are the target of the hyperboles pundit, catastrophizing can be really tough to handle when you find yourself caught up in it. This is when it is imperative to step back, take a deep breath, and try to put things into perspective. Oftentimes talking things over with a trusted confidant, spiritual advisor, or family member can help. Like the choice of camera angle, a different viewpoint will help you rise above defeatism and chart a course toward resolving the real issues.

Task of the week:

Catastrophizing is an emotionally immature behavior that leaders refuse to engage in. Simply put catastrophizing is the mark of a person who has not grown into full adulthood. Worse, this thought process also has attributes of manipulation attached as well.

Your drill this week is whenever you run into catastrophizing, find a solution. You needn't offer the solution in all instances; you can keep the thought to yourself, but your task is to look at the situations and determine an appropriate solution. For example, when touring the devastation of Pearl Harbor after the Japanese attack in 1941 Admiral Nimitz focused on the positive. He pointed out that the attack came on Sunday morning when most crewmen were on leave. Had the same ships been lured to sea and sunk while fully manned there would have been closer to 38,000 casualties rather than 3,800. Further, the Japanese had only attacked the American battleships, leaving the dry docks and fuel depots intact, a fact which he would leverage to massively speed up repairs and recovery. He was a leader who could see silver linings in the midst of the clouds of dejection, despair, and defeat.

Most folks are not self-starters. They want to be told what to do, especially in moments of crisis. This is where leaders excel. Leaders are able to point to a path because they refuse to be caught up in catastrophizing. For the next seven days focus on solutions not problems.

6. Personalization

> *"Don't take anything personally. Nothing others do is because of you. What others say and do is a projection of their own reality, their own dream. When you are immune to the opinions and actions of others, you won't be the victim of needless suffering."*
> Miguel Angel Ruiz[13]

Personalization is based around egocentricity; the entire world is shot through the prism of self. It is dysfunctional in many ways, not the least of which is that the self is usually found wanting. If the world revolves around a star player, for instance, it had better continue to do so or there will be trouble. Keeping things from becoming personal is not easy.

For example, if you have put in twenty years of martial arts training and a decade of teaching yet you have a parent telling you that little Timmy is not happy with the way you manage your class that's bound to get emotional. Do your best not to take it personally. This is how many people live their lives, pushing and prodding to get things just the way they want them to be, regardless of whether they actually know what is right or best about the subject at hand.

You find the same thing in most sports. If the Monday-morning quarterbacks on the sports shows criticize the coaches' decisions, it is their job. By the way, you do know that "Monday-morning quarterback" is a pejorative term, right? Don't take it personally. If they did not have something to complain about they wouldn't find anyone to watch their analysis. You may be your own worst critic, but you can also be your own fairest judge.

We recommend:

Listening. Yup, listening… and acknowledging the other person's concerns in a professional manner. We are not suggesting that you acquiesce to attempted steamrolling or complaints, but do listen.

The critic might actually have a point buried in their condemnation that you can use to become better. Those open to feedback virtually always benefit from it even though people giving their opinion don't often consider how hard it is for you to receive negative feedback objectively without hearing something positive as well. Taking the other person's comments or position personally, no matter how it comes across or how personal they attempt to make it, is of no benefit to you or your team. When faced with "constructive criticism," strive to look for the constructive and ignore the criticism.

Task of the week:

While the internet allows anyone with a narcissistic streak, a webcam, and limited inhibitions to act out inappropriately and have their proverbial 15 minutes of fame, leaders don't play that game. Certainly not with things that will come back to haunt them, but more generally leaders know that the world does not revolve around them. Leaders also know that other people don't wake up in the morning with their first thought being about how to mess with them and their world. With rare exceptions, people are just not that interested in you, they are more interested in themselves.

It's not about you. So, your drill this week is to not take things personally. For example, if your flight has been delayed or you've missed your connection, chances are good that you won't get very far with the agent at the ticket counter by saying, "You know this is very inconvenient for me." Try a different tact, saying something along the lines of, "Thank you for your help. I know this is difficult work and that you handle irate customers all day. I want you to know that I appreciate anything you can do to help me get to my destination on time."

Replace the frustration of the moment with the circumspect understanding of a leader that this is not about you. This week when you get cut off in traffic, your computer fails, or the mail carrier loses your package, bear in mind that it's not about you. At the end of the week, look at your biggest victory and your biggest moment of narcissism. How different are these moments? Which one was successful and which one was a failure?

7. External control

> "*My helplessness makes my uselessness seem unimportant.*"
> Wally (from the comic strip *Dilbert* by Scott Adams)[14]

Feeling externally controlled keeps you stuck. You do not believe you can really affect the basic shape of your life, let alone make any difference in the world. Believing that you have no control over your destiny creates a sense of helplessness and depression. It is easy to get down when outside forces appear to influence every aspect of your life. The aforementioned Filtering and Overgeneralization are culprits in this perceived ceding of control to others, however everyone makes decisions every day that affect their lives, hundreds of times a day in fact. Even prisoners. The challenge is recognizing those choices and placing them into the larger context.

We recommend:

At the micro level you will always have choices. Outside influences set a context and boundaries, but they cannot control everything. Break problems down into bite-sized chunks (see Chapter 10 for more information). Find the problem and seek a solution, but in small pieces. Find success with one item and use that accomplishment to build toward a larger goal.

Task of the week:

Leaders have the characteristic of not letting external events set their tone. They don't complain about things beyond their control. That does not mean they do not acknowledge what is transpiring around them, just that they recognize the context. Your task for this week is to observe peoples' conversations to take note of the energy that they place into the events and circumstances over which they have absolutely no control such as the weather or the performance of their favorite sports team. At the end of the week your attitude and your energy expenditure should have changed with no effort other than this observation.

8. Internal control

> *"Laws control the lesser man...*
> *Right conduct controls the greater one."*
> Mark Twain[15]

If you feel externally controlled, you see yourself as helpless, a victim of fate, but that's not the only distortion that can affect your sense of power and control. The second distortion is internal control. The fallacy of internal control has you responsible for the pain and happiness of everyone around you. It leaves you exhausted as you attempt to fill everyone else's needs and feel guilty when you cannot. A leader cannot do everything. You cannot simultaneously be mentor, counselor, friend, spiritual guru, financial advisor, dog-walker, and savior of everyone around you no matter how talented you are or how much you may feel inclined to try.

We recommend:

Know your limits. Good leaders are empathetic to those around them, particularly those in their care, but they can only do so much. You are responsible for fostering an environment where individuals can learn and grow, where talents are effectively utilized to further a superiorordinate goal (such as winning a championship or meeting company profit margins), and where everyone has the resources they need to be successful. You can assure communication, break down barriers, handle politics, acquire funding, train, and mentor, all things that help set folks up for success, but after that it's up to them. Learn to let go.

Task of the week:

Sitting and meditating is as old as man yet doing it around others can be a little awkward. We are going to add our spin to the centuries old practice to make it a little easier for you to accomplish both In public and in private. So, here is your mantra, "Control the body to control the mind; control the mind to control the body."

Here's how it works: You can sit anywhere, your office, your living room, even the back of a taxicab, and practice internal control. Sit completely still. Breathe in softly through your nose and exhale out through your mouth. Close your eyes if you want, but it's not necessary. Focus on your breathing and let it calm your mind. Thinking about nothing works great, but can also be a struggle for many. If you are one of them, try imagining a pool of clear, still water.

The more you calm your mind, the more your body will relax. This practice should be done whenever you remember to do it. Don't worry about a proscribed amount of time, use whatever you have available this week. Your goal is to build up a Pavlovian response where stillness equals calm. It may take more than seven days, but with practice this method will become almost effortless, allowing you to quickly reach a relaxed state simply by sitting perfectly still.

9. Fairness

> *"Life isn't fair, get used to it."*
> Unknown professor to college students in business class

You feel resentful because you think you know what's fair, but other people do not act that way (or agree with you). Fairness is so conveniently defined, so temptingly self-serving, that each person gets locked into his or her own point of view. It is easy to make assumptions about how things would change if people were truly fair or really valued you and your opinion. But if other people hardly ever see it that way you end up causing yourself a lot of pain and ever-growing resentment.

Look at the arguments around affirmative action for example. Pretty much everyone agrees that ending discrimination in hiring practices is a good thing, but disagreements pile up as to how to go about doing it. Are quotas best? Is there really such a thing as equal opportunity? Does addressing past wrongs resolve issues or draw them out? The list goes on… The point is that even when the goal is laudable, well-meaning people differ in approach and execution. Given that context, how likely is it that others will agree on what is fair from your knothole, let alone do all the things you would if you were in charge of everything?

If you find yourself getting worked up on certain topics, pay attention to your behavior. Are you turning into a sanctimonious jerk, mocking those who don't agree with you? Lord knows we've certainly done it from time to time. The challenge is that such behavior is not only unconstructive, it is downright detrimental. And, it affects everyone around you.

We recommend:

Have a baseball pitcher's mentality. In order to succeed at any level, pitchers need to have a short memory. If the pitcher is dwelling on the homerun he just gave up as the next batter is coming to the plate, well that pitcher has already lost the game. He is not living in the present moment. The greatest pitchers in Major League Baseball (MLB) history were adept at flushing the past and focusing on the future. Knowing that the only way to fix what had just happened was to let it go, they were able to move on to the next batter.

We like what MLB Hall of Fame member Ferguson Jenkins had to say, "Mental attitude and concentration are the keys to pitching." Take the right attitude. Let your moment of emotion go, just like the best pitchers do. Yes, it really is just that simple. And that challenging… Here's a little trick that can help. When you find yourself getting unduly wrapped up in emotion about a certain topic give yourself a timeout. It is time to stop. Take a deep breath, force yourself to relax, and change the subject.

The world is not fair, never has been, and almost certainly never will be. Have a short memory. Don't dwell on the past, learn, take the lesson, and move forward. Notice that we did not say move on, because "move on" is a dismissive. Don't be dismissive. Learn and move forward.

Task of the week:

For the next week, every time you find yourself feeling emotional about a subject say out loud, "I'm having an emotional reaction to this." Stop, take a deep breath, and think about why. We're not trying to turn you into a Vulcan, the emotionless race of aliens from the

Star Trek television and movie series, but we do want to assure that you are in touch with your hot buttons. This dovetails with flawed thinking around External Control. The world truly isn't fair, but that does not mean you should get upset about it.

10. Blaming

> *"We often spend our time and energy blaming other people for the problems we see around us."*
> Pearl Cleage[16]

Blame is a reverse action, to blame is to look to the past. As stated previously, leaders learn from the past but focus on the future. It is going to sound very simple, but while you can acknowledge responsibility, you cannot accept or lay blame.

Blame is a very low emotion. In blame systems, you deny your right and responsibility to assert your needs, say no, or go elsewhere for what you want. It's easy to do, commonplace, and very destructive. Blaming others makes someone else accountable for choices and decisions that are your responsibility.

We recommend:

Look for solutions instead of blame. It really doesn't matter why something went wrong except to the extent that you are able to identify a root cause in order to prevent it from happening again. Take responsibility for what you can control, find a way to resolve the issue, and flush the rest. Blame is unproductive.

Task of the week:

Look at yourself before you blame others this week. The root cause of an event could fall at the feet of another person, but your job is to look at what happened before pointing fingers or heaping blame upon yourself. The question you are to ask is, "What part of this am I responsible for? Is there a way I could have prevented this?" These are open-ended questions for an open mind.

11. Must

> *"Force always attracts men of low morality."*
> Albert Einstein[17]

The word "must" implies truth. If X is true, then Y must be false... Most things come with shades of grey, but not the word must. It is an imperative. Guard the word "must" with caution, using it only when appropriate, even in your own mind. It is easy to get wrapped up in what you must do if you set unreasonable expectations for yourself or others.

As a leader you have authority. Even if you are not in charge organizationally, whenever others look to you for guidance your word carries weight and simultaneously responsibility. If not well thought out, hard rules about how others must act can cause a horrible distortion of power.

For example, telling a martial arts student that he or she must lift their knee high in order to kick high truly is a must. The knee lift is imperative, it is physiologically impossible to kick high without doing it. Telling your spouse that the lawn be mowed every Tuesday between 1:00 pm and 2:00 pm, on the other hand, is a rule that may not have any basis in reason. It is unlikely to truly be a must. Telling a rookie professional athlete that he must guard his newfound wealth from hangers on who are attracted to his fame and fortune... well, it is not a must but it is darn good advice.

We recommend:

The word "must" should only be used when dealing with absolutes. When it comes to the grey areas of personal choices use phrases such as "I have found" or "It has been my experience" that provide leeway.

Task of the week:

How many musts do you create for yourself? And how many of those musts are casual? Think of it this way, how many times in your day-to-day conversation do you use the words "must", "need," or "have to" when it is truly not an imperative? It's easy to fall into that speech pattern habitually, so pay close attention to when you use the term must this week. Keep a small notepad and writing implement with you and make a tick mark each time you use the word must, then ask yourself, "Is it truly a must moment?" If not, choose alternate vocabulary.

12. Emotional reasoning

> *"I have a woman's body and a child's emotions."*
> Elizabeth Taylor[18]

Based on the theories of Carl Jung, Isabel Meyers and Katherine Briggs developed a model that breaks peoples' personalities down in to sixteen types. The Meyers-Briggs Type Indicator® (MBTI) they invented is one of the most widely used psychological instruments in the world. It uses scales to chart our natural predilections (see Brain Typing in Chapter 16 for more information).

One axis of the MBTI scale looks at "thinking" versus "feeling." This continuum examines how people make decisions. People who naturally gravitate towards thinking place a greater emphasis on objective data, whereas those with a tendency toward feeling are more likely to consider people and emotions when arriving at conclusions. These are natural tendencies based on your brain chemistry, hence neither right nor wrong, but they can cause challenges.

"My feelings are real!" Yes they are, but that does not necessarily mean that your feelings are valid or correct. Emotional statements often begin with the phrase, "I feel." When you find yourself saying or thinking the words "I feel" you are working from sentiment. Feelings are absolutely appropriate, but without some basis in fact it is easy for emotional reasoning to become irrational.

Take the phrase "Violence never solved anything" for instance. At its face it sounds pretty good, a heartfelt declaration against bloodshed and brutality, right? Unfortunately, the *only* way to resolve certain situations is through violence. Imagine what the Nazis would have done if no one had taken up arms against them.

Consistent, logical, and impersonal criteria are often best when weighing important decisions. For example, when it comes to strategic planning, be it in business, sports, or anything else, emotional reasoning just won't cut it. Emotions play an important role in selling ideas and gaining commitment, but if the underling plan simply makes everyone feel good more often than not it is bound to fail.

We recommend:

The phrase "I feel" is a tip off that your reasoning may not be valid. Examine the logic behind your thinking before making important decisions or acting on your thoughts. For some this is easy, whereas for others it gets crosswise with their natural predilections. If you are someone who falls into the latter category it may take some effort to realize when you are acting on emotion and ascertain whether or not it is in your best interests to do so for any given topic. This is where a trusted friend or family member can help. Find someone you trust completely, preferably one who tends more toward thinking than feeling by way of personality type, and ask him or her to work with you on this.

Task of the week:

This week listen to peoples' introductory statements to a moment or situation. If the sentence begins with the word "I" it is likely a position of emotion from which they are coming. Here is an example, "I found your words offensive." This is a statement about feelings. Alternately, "Those were poorly chosen words" describes the statement far less emotionally. By paying attention to how others behave it becomes easier to see similar behaviors in yourself. Carry a piece of paper or a notebook with you and draw tick marks on the page every time you use the phrase, "I feel." Becoming cognizant of how often you work from emotion should prove enlightening.

13. Resisting change

> *"Little men with little minds and little imaginations go through life in little ruts, smugly resisting all changes which would jar their little worlds."*
> Zig Ziglar[19]

While children can be pretty open-minded, adults tend to do whatever they do because it works for them. Their experience tells them that their decision is correct, even when it is not the best choice or even a constructive one. This is because most people fear transitions, hence are uncomfortable with genuine change. We all say the word "change," but what we often mean is "incremental adjustment." The reason that people do this is that we may not be able clearly envision ourselves in the future state. We might feel that our knowledge is inadequate, our skills are not applicable to the new situation, or that we do not have the experience necessary to succeed. Or, we might stubbornly cling to our comfort zones.

People do tend to be more willing to change given enough pain or pressure that the alternative of not changing is worse, but it is not natural for most to embrace transformation. In fact, forcing people to change when they have not bought in both emotionally and logically almost always breeds resentment. Worse, forcing change on yourself can cause second-guessing, angst, and discontentment. You can get stuck in your head even when you are sincerely trying to do the right thing.

We recommend:

If you are hoping to create change either for yourself or for your team, you will need to deal with this natural reluctance. This is often an extension of Emotional Reasoning. This means that you not only need to chart the course, explaining why the future state is desirable, but you must also demonstrate success quickly. Without proof that change can and will be successful, preferably with numerous small wins along the way, it is easy to revert back to the original state. Keep on top of it throughout the entire process, cajoling, counseling, navigating, or cheerleading as necessary.

Task of the week:

Step outside your comfort zone this week. The more often you challenge yourself to take risks the easier it will become to do so in the future. Given the speed of change in today's world, resistance to change is not only futile it's often self-destructive. You will miss out on vital opportunities.

It is easiest if you choose a worthwhile task that needs to be done so that your risk is meaningful. If you have a fear of heights, for example, go clean a gutter instead of paying someone else to do it. Or stand at the edge of an overlook with a sturdy guardrail and take photographs of the view. If public speaking is your great concern, find an opportunity to confront your fears and face a group. It is easier if you leverage your expertise, articulating something that you are intimately familiar with, so that giving the speech is your only challenge to overcome. These are just examples, pick something daring yet meaningful, embrace the opportunity to step beyond your comfort zone, and go make it happen.

14. Being right

> *"I'm always right. I thought I was wrong once but it turns out that I was mistaken."*
> Any drunk, on any bar stool, in every town

Humans are imperfect, we all make mistakes, yet some folks (probably most folks) are reluctant to admit it when they are the one who has made an error. Always having to be right is destructive in personal relationships. Ask anybody who is in a successful long term relationship and he or she will tell you about the give-and-take that is necessary. The same applies for your role as a mentor, teacher, or coach. Just because you are in a position of power does not mean that you are always right. We know that you already know that, but the challenge is what you do with it. When you're in charge and your reputation is on the line it is even tougher than normal to admit when you're wrong. But, it shouldn't be.

Listen to anyone who successfully coaches at a very high level (e.g., Major League Baseball, National Football League, or National

Basketball Association). They will publically admit whenever they have made a mistake. When things go right these coaches praise their team, whereas when things go wrong they take the blame, even if it is not really their fault. That is good policy and good leadership.

It sounds something like this, "Every pitcher wants to pitch, and they believe that their next pitch will resolve the situation, even when they're way behind the count. That is their nature and that is what we want. My mistake as a manager was that I left our star pitcher in for one pitch too long. That is why we lost 4 runs to 3. You just can't do that in the pros and I knew better…"

We recommend:

When you are wrong, or have made an error, quickly acknowledge and fix it. Words like, "I was wrong," "My mistake," or the hip, "My bad" are all ways to own up to the error. Willingness to admit mistakes is a sign of strength, not weakness. It may seem tough to admit a mistake, but the truly hard part is working to ensure it does not happen again. Apologizing is easy.

Task of the week:

This week let others be right. So long as their incorrect position does not threaten your organization or create some irrevocable form of loss, let it go. There is more than one way to do most everything; even if it's not the way you would do it yourself. Just because it is different does not necessarily mean that it is wrong, but for the next seven days it does not matter. If somebody wants to be wrong about something, there is no need to be the smartest person in the room and correct them.

15. Heaven's reward

> "Happiness is the reward we get for living
> to the highest right we know."
> Richard Bach[20]

We all want to be acknowledged. Fame and fortune have a certain allure, but the world really doesn't care about your work ethic, your hours in the weight room, the time you have invested to become a teacher, the degree(s) and certification(s) you have earned, or sacrifices you made to earn the martial arts rank that you have obtained. To assume that at some time you will be acknowledged and rewarded justly for your efforts is tantamount to building a house so that others can burn it down. That motivation simply makes no sense.

Leaders who put in the hard work and do the right things impact their organizations far more than most are ever acknowledged for, yet it is the right thing to do anyway. It boils down to intrinsic motivation, a fundamental trait of high achievers. If you choose to be a leader, you cannot get too wrapped up in whether or not you are credited for your efforts.

We recommend:

Sure, sometimes recognition does come with the job, but you cannot count on it. All you can really control is how and when you recognize others (see Chapter 17, Recognizing Effort, for strategies on doing that successfully). Set a good example and who knows, things may sort themselves out better than you expected.

Acknowledge the good stuff when it comes your way and do the things that satisfy you in a healthy manner. Create a healthy life. Because who is living your life, but you? Do not expect reward, but be thankful for it whenever it occurs.

Task of the week:

Do a good deed anonymously every day this week. Tell a coworker about the good job one of their employees has done, pay for someone else's coffee, donate to a worthy charitable organization, or write a positive online review for a product or service you enjoy. It can be something big or something small, but no matter what the effort is try to make it meaningful.

Sensei, Mentor, Leader, Coach Tip:

> Distorted thinking is as natural as breathing. The key is becoming aware of it. Knowing how and when your preconceived notions are dysfunctional allows you to minimize if not eliminate their impact.

Action:

This is one of those chapters you will likely need to refer back to repeatedly. Whenever you find yourself impacted by flawed thinking go to the relevant section and look toward our recommendations for mitigating the issue(s). Importantly, cut yourself some slack. You could easily go a lifetime without beating all of these tendencies, yet knowing what to look out for is more than half the battle. Diligently performing our tasks of the week should give you the awareness you need.

Stress exacerbates flawed thinking, so it is also important to be aware of what your body is telling you at any given time. In other words, being mindful of your physical stress response can help you regulate tension before it gets out of control. Think about how your body feels when you are stressed by your job, a personal relationship, money problem, or whatever brings you concern. How does it affect your breathing, muscle tension, digestion, or heart rate? Do you find yourself becoming angry or agitated, depressed or withdrawn? These are all warning signs to pay attention to. We cover burn out in more depth at the end of Chapter 17.

No matter what the cause, it is vital to find one or more stress-busting techniques to help minimize tension and clear your thinking. We talked about meditation earlier in this chapter (in the section on internal control), and there are many other options to consider as well. For example, if you are a visual person you may be able to relieve stress by surrounding yourself with uplifting images. If you respond more to sound, wind chimes, water fountains, or music can make a big difference. For kinesthetically inclined, exercise routines or sports, chopping firewood, or hitting a punching bag will help.

Sensei, Mentor, Teacher, Coach – Little Life Secret:

> Sometimes histrionics are necessary for people to get something off their chest, progress past the emotion, and move on to more productive things. Other times you need to snap them out of it. In those instances wait for them to wind down and then ask the question, "Why are you not taking action on this now?" Sometimes the act of having to own their words points out to people how extreme a position they have taken in a non-threatening manner.

5

THINKING BEYOND THE OBVIOUS

Three Principles to Utilize the Genius of Foolish Ideas

"The difference between a successful person and others is not a lack of strength, not a lack of knowledge, but rather a lack of will."
Vince Lombardi[21]

During World War II moving troops to meet the enemy was paramount. Drones did not exist back then and aircraft could only accomplish certain objectives, so without boots on the ground victory was impossible. Simple problem, hard solution... until Andrew Higgins came along. A boat builder from landlocked Nebraska, his innovation changed the course of the war. The Higgins boat he developed is the troop transport that famously hit the beaches at Normandy. Wave upon wave of these transports left their parent ships loaded with troops and headed for the beach as fast as they could go. Upon hitting the shoreline, the front gate dropped and 36 soldiers would scramble over the dunes into the fight.

While historians laud this innovation as instrumental to the war effort, at the time it almost did not happen. Higgins' offers to build the troop transport were rejected multiple times. The Navy could not get their heads around the shallow draft, spoonbill design, nor could they understand how a Nebraska native could be boat builder. Heck, Higgins was known to refer to the bow of his ships as "the front," clearly indicating that he was not a maritime man. But, he was a visionary.

Despite being rejected by the US Navy, Higgins knew in his heart that he was right, famously telling reporters, "The Navy doesn't know one damn thing about small boats." He also believed that his country was unnecessarily losing lives without his innovation, so he refused to give up. He approached another branch of the military—one that had the motto *Adapt, Overcome, Innovate*—the United States Marines. The Marines understood the value, embraced Higgins' design, and used his boats whenever possible. Although they were successful, those uses where sporadic. But, importantly, they got noticed.

Through the intervention of then Senator Harry S. Truman, Higgins was able to secure a head-to-head competition between his boat and the one the US Navy was using. Higgins' design crushed the rival's in every test—speed, maneuverability, capacity, etc. Under orders of the Truman Committee, the Bureau of Ships was forced to convert to the Higgins LCVP (Landing Craft, Vehicle and Personnel) boat, and do so immediately.

In a 1964 interview, President Dwight D. Eisenhower related, "Andrew Higgins is the man who won the war for us. If Higgins had not designed and built those LCVPs, we never could have landed over an open beach. The whole strategy of the war would have been different." Higgins' vision made the invasion of Normandy possible. The 23,398 LCVPs he designed and built changed the course of the war.

"Thinking outside the box" has become a trite, Dilbertesque statement that has lost much of its utility. We prefer the more inclusive "Thinking beyond the obvious." This simple change of phrase can make a profound shift in your mindset. It leads to the question, "What is obvious?" And, more importantly, "Does what is obvious really solve the problem?"

Let's take another example from history, the Spanish Civil War (which lasted from 1936 to 1939). General Francisco Franco, who would later rule Spain until his death in 1972, led the Spanish Nationalists against the established Spanish Republic. The Republic was supported by the Soviet Union, so they had access to a wide array of Soviet weaponry, including tanks. Consequently Franco was faced with the daunting task of designing a way to defeat a superior foe armed with far better military technology.

Put yourself in General Franco's head for a moment. You need to find a way to stop the adversary's tanks. How do you do it? Acquiring a larger number of tanks and trained crews to man them was virtually impossible, but there were several other options available including landmines, tank traps, WWI style berms and trenches, mortar shells, bazookas, etc. If you were Franco, what would you do?

If you are like us, you probably sat down and looked at mechanical solutions like those we listed above. After all, that's what precedent had shown effective in previous wars. General Franco, on the other hand, opted for a simple chemical solution. He took glass bottles, filled them with petrol, shoved a rag into the opening, and set them ablaze. Sound familiar? Yup, he invented the infamous Molotov cocktail. Franco was a brutal, ruthless dictator, and he was also a visionary.

Franco's troops lit their cocktails and tossed them in front of the invading tanks. Their goal was to have the tank drive over the conflagration so that it would get wound up in their treads. "Wait," you might say, "How did burning gasoline melt a metal tank tread?" It didn't; it actually melted the rubber wheels that the treads ran on, effectively giving the tank a flat tire despite the fact that the tread itself remained intact. This maneuver immobilized the enemy tanks.

Coach Lombardi in his quote that started this chapter said that it is the "will" that makes the difference between success and failure. True, but not having a smart will means not looking at all aspects of the problem. It just pushes harder on the predicament, irrationally expecting an improvement that may never come. That is the equivalent of General Franco telling his forces to shoot more bullets at the Soviet-built tanks. No matter how much lead they put into the air, it would not have penetrated the armor. In other words, shooting faster would have accomplished nothing more than wasting ammunition and pissing off the tank gunners.

All the effort in the world is worthless if it is not put to good effect. Similarly, if Higgins had come to the US military with a way to build the same old boats they were already using more efficiently at a lower cost it would have been equally worthless. Allied troops could not have stormed the beaches effectively and the world would in all likelihood be a very different place today.

Thinking beyond the obvious is based on looking past the established paradigm. It truly is working smarter, not harder. Volumes have been written on how to go about doing that, but in practical reality it boils down to three things: (1) Understanding your goal, (2) Seeking solutions and information outside the norm, and (3) Employing diversity of thought. Seems simple, perhaps overly so, but let's elaborate:

1.   Understanding your goal

What are you truly trying to accomplish? The old saw goes that we never have time to get it right, but we can always find time to do it again. Solving the wrong problem quickly makes no sense, yet it is oftentimes the norm, particularly in bureaucratic organizations.

The way the goal is stated tends to drive the solution, so be sure to cut to the heart of the matter before you apply resources toward resolving it. This may take extra time and exploration, but it is well worth the effort. In the Spanish Civil War example, are you trying to blow-up the enemy tank or are you trying to disable it? Does the tank actually need to be destroyed in order to meet your objective? Franco's goal was probably something along the lines of "Prevent the enemy from using his tanks against me" as opposed to "Find a way to destroy the enemy tanks," which presupposes a suboptimal solution.

The better you can articulate the problem the more effectively you can design a solution to resolve it. There are multiple tools that can help such as the root cause analysis, straw man concept, storyboarding technique, affinity diagram, cause and effect analysis, four-frame approach, interrelationship diagram, and the like. The method you choose is far less important than the outcome.

One of the simplest and most effective ways to cut to the heart of a problem is the 5 Whys technique. Popularized in the 1970s via the Toyota Production System, this strategy involves looking at any problem and asking: "Why?" or "What caused this?" Oftentimes the answer to the first "why" will prompt another "why" and the answer to the second will prompt another and so on, hence the name. In this fashion you not only assure that you're solving the right thing, but also that you can explain the problem in a manner that is likely to drive a successful solution.

2. Seeking solutions and information outside the norm

Groupthink is a tendency within organizations (or societies) to promote or establish the view of the predominant group. It can be dysfunctional not only because it tends to squash innovation, but also because it downplays individual creativity and personal responsibility in favor of the collective norm.

There is a Japanese expression, "The nail that sticks up gets pounded down." If there is only one "right" way to do things, few people will take the risk to attempt anything different. Some of us are willing to take risks, happy to ask for forgiveness rather than permission, but if organizational norms do not provide leeway for measured risk-taking it will become a very rare thing. We discuss the four elements of creating culture in Chapter 7; refer to this for more information.

Blues guitarist Jeff Healey (1966 – 2008) was blind. He learned to play the guitar in his lap, because nobody told him he couldn't do it that way. Going outside the norm can facilitate similar innovation. If you are a machinist trying to redesign a tool, you should read what an artist has to say. If you are an athlete trying to speed up your 40-yard dash, consider how an engineer might approach the challenge. Sometimes the accepted way of doing things is the optimal solution, but more often than you might think it is not.

It's not just who you talk to, but also how you ask. Oftentimes we attempt to resolve sticky situations by searching for the root cause of our problems, yet flipping things around to look at what is going right can be a better approach in many instances. This tactic is commonly called "appreciative inquiry." It helps build on our strengths, just as conventional problem-solving can help manage or eliminate our weaknesses.

Appreciative inquiry follows a five step process to (1) Define the challenge, (2) Perform discovery, (3) Dream of what's possible, (4) Design a solution, and (5) Deliver results.

1. **Define**: before you can analyze a situation, you need to define what you are looking for. Rather than describing a problem, however, look for the positive aspects instead. For example, seek "Ways to improve our offensive productivity" as opposed to determining "Why we are not scoring enough points." Your choice of wording can make a big difference; rather than constraining your line of inquiry, your definition should open the option to explore possibilities.
2. **Discovery**: seek to understand what has happened before and the best of what is working well now. Design your questions broadly, open-end inquiries that can get subject matter experts talking about proud moments, successes to build upon. Factors that contributed to the team or organization's past successes can be leveraged to build the future. Seek them out.
3. **Dream**: brainstorm what might be. Think about how you can leverage current positives and reinforce them to build lasting strengths. Oftentimes this will simultaneously clarify things you need to stop doing in order to progress or areas where you can repurpose resources to invest in the future you wish to create. Nevertheless, start with the possible before delving into the practical so that you do not overly constrain your thinking.
4. **Design**: this is where you begin the process of turning the dream into reality, designing discrete changes to processes, tools, systems, strategies, and/or personnel to make it real. Identify what it takes to enable the dream and chart the course to get there. Depending on the scope and complexity of what you are attempting this may require a resource-loaded project plan, though oftentimes it's much simpler than that.

5. **Deliver**: implement the plan. While turning your design into reality is the primary focus, it is important to consider appreciative inquiry a continuous process. In delivering results be open-minded to re-evaluate and continue the process of positive change.

It is intuitively obvious to most that groupthink is not a good thing, yet it takes conscious effort to avoid falling into its trap. Seeking solutions outside the norm is vital for continuous improvement, without which we and our organizations cannot remain competitive (or even relevant in many cases) over the long run.

3. Employing diversity of thought

This is an extension to previous point, but gets more to the thought process than the organizational norm. For example, if you are a man speak to a woman, if you are a woman talk to a man. It is no secret that the genders see the world in different ways. Leveraging this diversity can be powerful.

Going a bit deeper, consider personality types such as described by the Myers-Briggs Type Indicator® (MBTI), Insights® Wheel, Herrmann matrix, and the like, and make a concerted effort to hold discussions with folks who think and process information differently than you do. If you are unfamiliar with these models, don't sweat the details now, we go into more specificity when we discuss brain typing in Chapter 16. While we are partial to the MBTI, all of these templates provide useful ways to understand differences in cognitive process so that you can collaborate with others more effectively.

For example, Kane is an ENTJ using the MBTI model. The acronym ENTJ stands for Extravert, iNtuitive, Thinking, Judgmental, which is a summary of where a person lands on the nexus of four continua. People with this personality type tend to be solution-oriented, strategic thinkers. They are frank, decisive, and forceful, sometimes overly so, as they have a bias for action and oftentimes like to be in charge. Balancing this with a more explorative personality type such as an INFP (Introvert, iNtuitive, Feeling, Perceiving) can help assure a fuller exploration of options.

Surrounding yourself with people who think differently than you do can be a catalyst for identifying and implementing innovative ideas, something that rarely happens without diversity of thought. A great way to take this to the next level is to leverage modern technology to reach out to others through the phenomena of crowdsourcing. In this fashion you can obtain information and input by harnessing the creative energy of large numbers of people, casually interested parties and stakeholders alike, through the internet by using social media, collaboration tools, SharePoint sites, wikis, and the like. See Chapter 13, cross-pollination, for more information.

Sensei, Mentor, Teacher, Coach Tip:

> The more educated and experienced we get the less creative we oftentimes become as we gravitate again and again toward the "right" answer, even if it's the same answer we have used countless times before. Innovation is not always necessary, but developing a mindset that allows you to think beyond the obvious can help set you and your team apart from your competition.

Action:

If you find yourself saying or thinking, "We have always done it that way," it is best to consider why you have done so. If the circumstances are the same, great, but if they have changed, a common enough occurrence, the old solution may be suboptimal at best. Strive to surround yourself with people who have divergent backgrounds and experience as well as those who process information differently than you do. By understanding your goal, seeking solutions and information outside the norm, and employing diversity of thought you can come up with far better outcomes than you thought possible.

While most folks easily fall into a pattern of habitual decision-making, even silly stuff like salting their food before tasting it, if you want to think beyond the obvious it is important to get creative in all aspects of your life. For example, if you've ever eaten breakfast at Denny's, IHOP, or the like you've no doubt seen a menu choice of "3 eggs, any style." What's your favorite, over-easy? Scrambled?

Hard boiled? How about ordering three different options? After all, it doesn't say "3 eggs all cooked the same," right? Whether they're your favorites or not, have you even considered the possibility of ordering one over-easy, one scrambled, and one hardboiled egg?

Start training your mind to think beyond the obvious today. Consider books such as *The Lean Startup: How Today's Entrepreneurs Use Continuous Innovation to Create Radically Successful Businesses* by Eric Ries, *The Four Steps to the Epiphany* by Steve Blank, *Ten Types of Innovation: The Discipline of Building Breakthroughs* Larry Keeley, et. al., or *Out Think: How Innovative Leaders Drive Exceptional Outcomes* by G. Shawn Hunter. Read at least one title like these every two or three months as time permits. In hearing other's stories it oftentimes becomes easier to recognize our own.

Book learning is nice, it gets the creative juices flowing, but it's vital to keep it real too. Find out what other people in your organization are doing right. Identify an innovative leader you respect, preferably someone whose area of responsibility is different than your own so that you are not directly competing with each other, and ask about mentoring opportunities. By spending a few hours a month with someone who knows your organization's culture and is adept at creating transformation from within it, you can create tremendous synergy, giving both your teams an advantage.

When possible form or join a community of practice to facilitate teaming and thought leadership within and beyond your organization. Make contact with creative individuals with whom you can share success stories, failures, and best practices.

Sensei, Mentor, Teacher, Coach – Little Life Secret:

> Sometimes people are so locked into a way of thinking that they need to fail in order to learn and grow. As a leader it is your responsibility to limit the damage and, without saying "I told you so," move forward to a better plan while keeping the end goal in mind.

DON'T FEAR EXPECTATIONS

Five Ways to Kill Fear and Move Forward

"Don't lower your expectations to meet your performance. Raise your level of performance to meet your expectations. Expect the best of yourself, and then do what is necessary to make it a reality."
Ralph Marston[22]

In Paris, France at the Sorbonne, the historical house of the University of Paris, Teddy Roosevelt gave a speech titled *Citizenship in a Republic*. The speech is over one hundred years old and carries these famous words now referred to as, "The Man in the Arena." An excerpt follows:

> *"It is not the critic who counts; not the man who points out how the strong man stumbles, or where the doer of deeds could have done them better. The credit belongs to the man who is actually in the arena, whose face is marred by dust and sweat and blood; who strives valiantly; who errs, who comes short again and again, because there is no effort without error and shortcoming; but who does actually strive to do the deeds; who knows great enthusiasms, the great devotions; who spends himself in a worthy cause; who at the best knows in the end the triumph of high achievement, and who at the worst, if he fails, at least fails while daring greatly, so that his place shall never be with those cold and timid souls who neither know victory nor defeat."*

Expectations are often feared because they mean that you may fail. But if you never try you will fail nonetheless. Since you are reading this book you are undoubtedly already aware of this need. You want to be exceptional, right? However, it is often the case that we allow expectations to be managed or negotiated such that they regress to the mean and in doing so we are made average.

Phrases like "It's too hard," "How is anybody expected to know this," or other familiar forms of lowering expectations are so commonplace that one could almost consider them institutionalized. Those who do set high expectations, set lofty goals, and manage their lives toward accomplishing them are oftentimes ridiculed by those who have no goals or low aspirations—precisely what Teddy Roosevelt was talking about in the quote above.

Stay with us for a minute while we touch on a piece of developmental biology called the morphogenetic field. This field is based on the idea that localized biochemical interactions or signals lead to the development of specific structures such as organs. Space and time of an embryonic field are dynamic, but they are defined by the field in which the cell inhabits. In other words, the morphogenetic field for a kidney only allows the cells to become kidneys. Likewise the heart is only allowed to become a heart when those cells are within the heart field.

Now we know that's a little bit of science theory and all, but how many times have you as a leader had an opportunity to define a vision through expectations for student, employee, or athlete and watch them grow into that position? In many ways your role as a mentor, teacher, or coach is the same as the morphogenetic field. When you set expectations and make them obtainable through coaching, tutelage, and education, the student, employee, or athlete is able to grow into the field that you have defined.

If you set a small field they will only grow to the edge of it. In other words, with rare exceptions those in your charge will only grow as big as the vision and the expectations you set for them. By setting low expectations you get low results. By setting high expectations, they (and you) can reach for so much more. Success is never assured, but with the right goals and coaching you can rest assured that they will not live in a world that never knows neither victory nor defeat, but have a real chance to accomplish something great.

Sounds terrific, but without a mechanism it can be tough. The good news is that there is a tool that has proven successful, the SMART goal-setting process. It has been around for a very long time and is widely adopted in Fortune® 500 companies because it works so well. The acronym SMART stands for (1) Specific, (2) Measurable, (3) Achievable, (4) Relevant, and (5) Time-bound. Here's how it works:

1. **Specific:** the goal is stated in precise terms and describes a deliverable or outcome. A specific goal has a greater impact than a general objective and is not only much more likely to be accomplished, but easier to know when you have done so.
2. **Measurable:** what gets measured gets done. Progress toward the goal can be tracked using standards, specifications, milestones, and the like such that you know when/if you have met it.
3. **Achievable:** the goal provides a motivational stretch so that it is a challenge to accomplish yet possible to achieve. If a goal is too far out of reach, you may become discouraged hence unable to maintain the energy or commitment necessary to achieve it. In such instances carve the end game into manageable chunks and set those smaller goals along the path to success.
4. **Relevant:** Tying the goal to something that is important to you will help assure a wholehearted commitment toward achieving it. The goal must also be aligned with the team or organization's purposes such that the individual's aspirations support the larger effort and not move at cross-purposes. This is vital not only for teaming, but also for acquiring necessary support and resources.
5. **Time-bound:** Tracking your progress over time assures forward momentum and builds in the opportunity to celebrate wins and/or course-correct along the way. The goal should include milestones that determine whether or not you are making progress against a reasonable schedule.

Sensei, Mentor, Teacher, Coach Tip:

> As the old saying goes, people seldom hit what they do not aim for. Given the right opportunity, most people step up (or sadly down) to expectations. Setting lofty yet achievable goals for yourself and those in your charge affords an opportunity to grow. It is far better to aim at a goal and fail, then to never aim and have a mouth full of worthless, "Could haves," "Would haves," and "Should haves."

Action:

Utilize the SMART process to define specific, measurable, achievable, relevant, and time-bound goals for yourself and others. Track progress and meet regularly to discuss how things are going, adjusting as necessary to stay on course.

Extrinsic motivation (inspiration from others) is great to have, yet intrinsic (self) motivation is essential for long-term development, particularly as you reach plateaus along the way where you may struggle for a period of time without perceptible progress. Publilius Syrus was a poet and philosopher who lived somewhere around 46 BC. A native of Syria, he was brought to Italy as a slave yet won his freedom and education by impressing his master with his talent and wit. He has a famous quote which is apropos here, "Do not turn back when you are just at the goal."

This advice seems sort of obvious, but when it comes to overcoming significant roadblocks in obtaining lofty goals all too many folks give up and turn back. This is where the SMART process, when put in place with forethought and planning, becomes most powerful.

Sensei, Mentor, Teacher, Coach – Little Life Secret:

> Start early. If your child envisions college from a very early age, chances are good he or she will make it there one day. If new employees see themselves on a career path, they are more likely to continuously acquire skills and experience necessary for success than someone who has merely found a job.

7

CONTEXT IS CRITICAL

Four Elements of Creating Culture

> *"I've missed more than 9,000 shots in my career. I've lost almost 300 games. 26 times, I have been trusted to take the game winning shot and missed. I've failed over and over and over again in my life. And that is why I succeed."*
> Michael Jordan[23]

Google Executive Chairman Eric Schmidt predicted that the world's entire population will be on the internet by 2020. The genie is out of the bottle and anybody who wants to see, pattern, or emulate what others have created has virtually no barrier to entry save for the most capital intensive of endeavors. Content, content, content. If it's been written, filmed, or even thought about it's probably out there somewhere. There is so much content that we are practically drowning in it. The vital aspect that you provide as a mentor, teacher, or coach is applying context to that content.

Context is extremely important. For example, if a 240 pound high school senior raced across the lunchroom on a Wednesday, lowered his shoulder, and slammed his body into a 160 pound sophomore driving him onto the ground and giving him a serious concussion, we would likely have lawsuit in the making, right? Editorials would be written, fingers would be pointed, blame would be laid, and the perpetrator would be expelled. Teachers, administrators, and parents would do all kinds of hand-wringing and asking, "Why?" and, "How could this horrific violent act happen?" Programs would likely put in place to help assure that it would never happen again... Assuming that all happened in the lunchroom. Or the classroom, courtyard, or parking lot... But, what if that exact same event took place on a Friday night under the lights of the football field? Suddenly the scenario is completely different. Context is everything.

Of course in most things context tends to be a bit more nuanced than our previous illustration. Take martial arts by way of example. Of all the sports one can participate in, martial arts are unique. More dynamics are in play than in other endeavors. People get involved in the arts for reasons that range from getting enough exercise to learning self-protection to obtaining spiritual enlightenment. Consequently those crafting a martial arts program must take into consideration how best to serve their students' needs, teach skills that are by their very definition warlike and dangerous, and simultaneously address the legal, moral, ethical, and historical aspects of the knowledge they choose to impart. It can be a significant challenge.

Unfortunately the majority of people are overly-focused on the content. Teaching how to punch and kick without considerations for the legal aspects of self-defense is like showing someone how to drive a car without ever explaining the rules of the road. It is incumbent upon martial arts instructors to look to the context of what they do. And, to set the culture in doing it.

All too often we hear an instructor proudly proclaim we do [insert name of a martial system here] in a tone that makes it clear what he or she is really declaring is that, "We have the secrets, and not only do we have the secrets we have the best secret secrets that were ever kept secret from all of you losers out there who don't have access to our über-secret secrets." Perhaps they do have secrets, legitimately. Most systems do to some small degree, but let's face it, all styles teach largely similar content due to the simple fact that there are only so many ways that the body can move and only a certain number weak spots that can be exploited to control or hurt someone. What's truly unique, where exclusivity actually exists, is history and context, the lens through which the content is offered.

In this fashion context is used to create and maintain culture, a state where members of the group feel shared pride of membership.

They dress alike, speak similarly, share a common history, and so on. We are not talking cult behavior here, though that can be an extreme example, but rather the sense of belonging one might find with just about any social club, fraternity, or sports team. In such groups there is order, hierarchy, values, and cultural norms. There can also be a social or corporate framework that wraps around it.

Humans are social animals, each of us with a strong sense of belonging that is essential to our mental, and oftentimes physical, well-being. Membership brings order. Everyone needs a role, a definition of where and how they fit into society. Belonging is so important, in fact, that virtually all humans would rather be a marginally tolerated member, the least of any group, than not belong to one at all.

Think the desire to belong isn't powerful? Consider this: as a species humans have a strong survival instinct. Few folks capable of rational thought would voluntarily throw themselves onto a hand grenade set to explode, sprint through a minefield, or carry a wounded compatriot out of a raging battle under great personal risk, yet those very examples happen over and over again in times of war. One of the underlying reasons is that soldiers build bonds by training together, deploying together, and facing horrific violence as a team, so much so that the fear of being thought a coward by one's comrades-in-arms overrides the natural instinct toward self-preservation.

Being ostracized puts a person in complete and utter limbo. After some tragedy occurs how many times do we see someone who knew the perpetrator shake their head and sadly relate to a journalist, "He just couldn't find his place in the world"? Even loners feel a need to get along; those who cannot oftentimes lash out in unexpected ways.

Think about the Rwandan genocide that took place In the early 1990s. According to government census reports 1,074,017 people, approximately one-seventh of the total population of Rwanda, were killed. Men, women, children, and even infants, were chopped to bits with machetes, their bodies left to rot in the sun. It's hard to imagine the gruesome sights, sounds, and smells let alone consider the minds of those who participated in such depravity.

How could something so terrible occur? Virtually all of the perpetrators who were interviewed after those events related that they would have rather have committed the atrocities than risk being laughed at or shunned by their friends and neighbors for not taking part in the carnage.

Shunning is the act where a group of people cuts off all contact with an individual who was once a member of the assembly. From a point in time forward, no one will acknowledge the shunned person's existence in any way through written word, speech or gesture. It is the complete opposite of membership, an act so powerful that in the right context it can actually kill.

While banishment from ancient tribes was for all intents and purposes a death sentence, shunning can still be effective today, both in the developed and developing worlds, though for the most part it is not nearly as powerful as it once was. The Amish, for instance, use the threat of ostracism to keep people in line with their rules of order much as certain religious institutions use the potential of excommunication. Nevertheless, safety nets for essential services exist today that were not available in the past. If an Amish person was kicked out of his or her community, for instance, that person could seek assistance elsewhere, whether it is social services, job training, or even the possibility of membership in another church group, yet they would still lose contact with all of their friends and family. It is not just physical health that is threatened by such acts, but mental wellbeing as well. Think about how hard it would be to transplant your life to another area where you do not know anyone and have no safety net.

This is where content cannot help. As a martial arts instructor you set the context and help shape the future of those around you. You have the responsibility to take into account the fact that you are providing not only the martial arts content, but the context, which is far more powerful than the actual martial act. Similarly, business leaders, teachers and mentors have a powerful role in shaping their organizations. Through words and deeds they impact the mental

Context is Critical

and physical security of those in their charge. Context is vital for setting culture.

The four aspects of creating and sustaining culture include (1) Commitment, (2) Community, (3) Clarity, and (4) Communication. Here's how they work:

1. **Commitment**: this means being bound emotionally and intellectually to a course of action. It is far more powerful, and sustainable, than mere compliance. People need to believe in the mission, vision, and direction of the team or organization and be willing to align their goals to help achieve it (this is discussed in depth in Chapter 11 where we cover personal and organizational mission and vision statements). Even when you have hierarchical authority, the ability to hire and fire, you cannot force commitment. What you can do is create a vision, help folks see themselves in the bigger picture, tie their success to the organization's success, and thoughtfully discuss any concerns or misgivings.
2. **Community:** leaders obviously do not act alone. Anyone with a position or responsibility that affects or is affected by the culture plays a role. Sometimes dissenters can become your biggest advocates. If you can bring them into your vision, show them its value and how they fit, and get them wholeheartedly on board others will see and follow their example. Reformed naysayers often become the biggest proselytizers. Be sure to identify and engage people emotionally where they live, align them with roles that give them the best chance of success (see Brain Typing in Chapter 16 for more information), and incentivize them to work together.
3. **Clarity:** people cannot work toward something they do not see or understand. To gain commitment they must envision a path to success (we cover Tackling Insurmountable Challenges in the next chapter). Explain the steps involved, how risks will be managed, what support will be provided, and what benefits will result from getting there. As the old saying goes, people who have a "why" will accomplish almost any "how."

4. **Communication**: this sort of goes without saying, but leaders must be effective communicators in order to have any shot at success. You can have a great vision, but if folks cannot understand what you are trying to convey they cannot buy in. This can be especially challenging for certain personality types. If you are one of them, consider taking classes on communication techniques, acquiring a mentor, or leveraging groups such as Toastmasters International (www.toastmasters.org) to improve your skills.

It takes more than just training, coaching, or lecturing to create and sustain culture. Feedback is a two-way street, assure robust discussion and interplay such that affected folks can viscerally understand. Avoid pure facts and data; strive to incorporate story-telling, anecdotes, and narratives in order to connect emotionally with your audience (see Chapter 15, The Right Words, for more information).

Whenever possible you must provide opportunities for stakeholders to experience, support, and help build the culture too. Folks own what they create, even when they only play a small role in the development process.

Sensei, Mentor, Teacher, Coach Tip:

> Leaders cannot afford to have a bad day. Sure, everyone is up or down at times, but when you're the person in charge everything that you say or do is scrutinized by those around you, especially your subordinates. You may have the power to hire and fire, hold the purse strings, or just be a well-respected thought-leader, but either way your opinion counts. Know that you have a position of authority and hold this in your mind as you work through your day. What example are you setting?

Action:

Think about the messages, intentional and unintentional, that your actions convey. What are you doing to the culture, the physical well-being, and the emotional health of those you interact with? You cannot script every moment of your life, but you can pledge to become more aware of the messages you send. Make a concerted effort to set the example intentionally.

For example, you might be late for a meeting, task-focused, or otherwise mentally checked out as you walk down a hallway past one of your subordinates or coworkers and fail to acknowledge their nod of hello. Missed the greeting, right? "No big deal," you might think, "She knows I value her as a team member." Wrong! To you it may not be a big deal, but your team member will likely spend the rest of the day wondering why you are mad at them.

A useful tool is the Stop-Start-Continue exercise. Typically administered by a non-advocate facilitator or human resources professional to assure anonymity of inputs, the team is asked to identify behaviors they would like you to stop doing, actions they would like you to take, and meritorious conduct to continue in order to be a better leader. Perform this exercise with your team, listen to the feedback, and make a concerted effort to act on what you hear. This should not be a onetime deal, follow-up every six months to a year or so to track your progress. It helps keep you humble and open to constructive feedback while setting a great example for your team.

Sensei, Mentor, Teacher, Coach – Little Life Secret:

> A smile actually changes your demeanor. To truly make the smile effective, however, you need to squint slightly as real smiles goes all the way into your eyes. Try it; you will feel an instant change in your attitude. Sometimes this is all you need to do in order to avoid having your bad day adversely affect those around you.

8

TACKLING INSURMOUNTABLE CHALLENGES

Eight Steps to Achieving the Impossible

"Even within the band, if I cannot manage to persuade the members of what I see to be the next course of action, how do you expect the group to deal with the expectations of thousands of people? It is not possible."
Robert Fripp[24]

If the task at hand is seen as impossible, such as defeating a much larger team, stealing work away from an entrenched competitor, earning a black belt, or defeating a superior rival, nothing you say or do will make a difference to the people you lead. Your comments, your policy, your ideas will be dismissed out of hand, likely not publicly but in the hearts and minds of your team for certain. To build a path to success, you must be credible, honest, and have a plan that opens the door to your vision. And, of course, you must also gain the agreement from your team to follow that roadmap.

Wilder, while working on a political campaign, discovered that the committee had become burdened with a large amount of debt early in the primary season. This early liability was poison. He knew that a campaign in debt could dissolve quickly as an entity, leaving no means for vendors to recoup their losses. When a political campaign does not have enough money to pay its debts, experienced suppliers refuse to extend credit as they know that campaigns are notorious for defaulting on their obligations. From long experience they know that campaign managers often walk away, clap the metaphorical dust from their hands, and say, "That's not my problem," while the supplier loses their proverbial shirt.

Faced with this situation, the Finance Director stood in front of the staff and declared, "We are going to look this green-eyed monster straight in the eyes and deal with it." Then he shifted subjects and began to talk about the candidate's vision, offering not a single actionable item the team could use for resolving the debt crisis. Clearly nobody believed him. Within a week all the key staff members had abandoned the campaign, finding safer work elsewhere. The Director's message had not met the group's needs. It failed to honestly address the issues at hand, was not perceived as credible, and was singularly unsuccessful in building a bridge to success that staffers could see themselves accomplishing.

Sports teams address issues like this with virtually every game. For example, if a Division II collegiate football team is pitted against a Division I opponent, the Division II team is almost certainly going to be outmatched man-for-man in athletic ability. Nevertheless, the coaches do not give up. They put together a game plan the recognizes the mismatch, addresses the weaknesses head on, and plays to whatever strengths they have to give them a chance, no matter how slight, at a victory. The team meeting might sound something like this:

"You can see by the film why their running back is a Heisman candidate. You can also see that they love throwing the ball deep. That quarterback's got a rocket for an arm. Gentleman, this is not going to be easy. They are a very, very good team and they have national championship aspirations. To put us in a position to have any chance to win we cannot let them score early and often. We need to play them close so that we're still in it late in the game. To do that, we are going to have to control the clock. We'll start with a combination of outside running and short passes…"

Will the Division II team win? Maybe, maybe not. After all, if statistics were the only thing that mattered there would not be any reason to play the game. Even consensus number one teams are beaten by unranked opponents from time to time. To have a shot at victory, no matter how slight, the coach had to lay out a vision and build a bridge for getting there that his players could believe in. Though resolving a team issue calls for different tactics than addressing an individual challenge, this approach works in virtually any situation.

Take a more personal example: we have a student at our *dojo* who was born with cerebral palsy. As a result he has limited control of some of his extremities. Given these constraints the student, let's call him Smith, was frustrated with his lack of performance. The first question that Wilder asked himself upon recognizing the issue was whether or not it was something that he should attempt to resolve. Not every problem can be addressed by the teacher, mentor, or coach, nor should it be, but in this instance Wilder felt that it was his place to get involved.

Wilder was suspicious that the other kids had diminished Smith's perception of his value as a person. Kids, especially those of Smith's age, can be petty and cruel. That's common enough. While cruelty from one's peers can be a powerful blow to one's self-esteem, succeeding in the face of adversity can build it up beyond measure. That is why Wilder felt the need to step in.

There was a significant upside to setting this kid up for success, yet making the decision to get involved was not enough. Before he could chart a course toward resolution, Wilder had to be sure that he understood the extent of the challenges that his student faced. He spoke privately with the young man's parents to find out more information, asking things like:

- "What did the doctors say?"
- "What was Smith already doing to help himself?"
- "What were the parents doing?"
- "How were all these items working?"

During this conversation he discovered that Smith has less than perfect control of his body and that his challenge was never going to go away. Likewise, make sure you have enough information to define the problem, cut to the core of the issues, and place boundaries around whatever it is you are trying to resolve. You don't need all the information, but you do need enough for prudent planning and decision-making.

Armed with a reasonable understanding of the problem and its root cause, Wilder began to build the bridge. He pulled Smith aside after class one night and said, "You have Cerebral Palsy. It is not going away, we both know that. You really have two choices, you can just roll over and let it hold you down or you can choose to excel. If you choose to excel you are going to have to work harder than anybody else in the *dojo*. It isn't fair and it won't be easy. What you are doing right now is not good enough to succeed, but if you are in, if you are willing to put forth the effort, I will help you. Are you in? Yes or no?"

The kid responded with, "Yes I'm in." Knowing that achieving noticeable early results would start to build a path of success, Wilder then went on to list specific actions for Smith to take to assure that he would be as productive as possible.

Change is hard. Making substantive improvements for a person with a significant disability like the karate student with cerebral palsy, or turning around a failing organization or sports team is often seen as insurmountable. King Whitney Jr., head of the National Urban League, put that into perspective when he said:

> *"Change has a considerable psychological impact on the human mind. To the fearful it is threatening because it means that things may get worse. To the hopeful it is encouraging because things may get better. To the confident it is inspiring because the challenge exists to make things better."*

As the quote indicates, confidence is the key to making things better. But, how can you be confident if you have not done it before or have struggled in the past? Like most things, there is a process. By taking the right steps in the proper order you can increase your odds of achievement. The necessary elements for creating lasting change include (1) Urgency, (2) Coalition, (3) Vision, (4) Buy-in, (5) Empowerment, (6) Progress, (7) Follow-through, and (8) Success. Here's how the process works:

1. **Urgency**: begin by communicating a sense of urgency. Help others see the need for change, the value proposition, what's in it for them, and why action is needed now. Without urgency your plan will continuously risk getting out-prioritized by more important things. Lack momentum and nothing new materializes because it is so easy to revert to the original state.

2. **Coalition**: create a guiding coalition. Assemble a group of stakeholders or thought-leaders with enough clout to get things done. In businesses this is likely to be a steering committee of folks with organization and budget authority, but oftentimes it can be impassioned individuals who are willing to champion the cause as a team. For individual change this is often a support group, counselor, advisor, or specialist who has expertise necessary to help.
3. **Vision**: create a vision to direct the effort. Oftentimes in business this is a formalized statement of direction backed up by specific goals, objectives, and timelines. A cogent and pithy vision makes all the difference in setting yourself up for success. We talk about mission and vision statements in Chapter 11, and goal setting in Chapter 6. Formality aside, the clearer you can define the problem and prospective solution the better. See Chapter 5, Thinking Beyond the Obvious, for more information on how to do that.
4. **Buy-in**: achieve broad buy-in for the vision. Make sure that as many stakeholders as possible understand and accept the strategy. While a leader or executive team can levy tasks, folks are far more likely to embrace the challenge if they play a role in developing and implementing the solution. Coopting naysayers within the organization, whenever possible, is a fantastic method of soliciting support. It takes time and personal relationships to do so, but is almost always worth the effort.
5. **Empowerment**: empower broad-based actions. Remove obstacles to change, attacking systems or structures that could undermine the vision you hope to implement. Encourage measured risk-taking and nontraditional solutions that further the cause (see Chapter 5, Thinking Beyond the Obvious, for more information). For process, rules-centric, or bureaucratic organizational cultures, it is paramount that the team has the authority necessary to make needed changes. Be sure that key decision-makers sponsor and support the effort. When working on individual change it sometimes helps to make a "contract" with your advisor(s) such that you feel compelled to understand and accept their counsel even if you are uncomfortable with what you hear.

6. **Progress**: generate quick wins. Make sure the plan has milestones that can be celebrated and recognize the folks who were involved in achieving them (see Chapter 17, Recognizing Effort, for more information). Have a communication plan too; the more visibility of success, the better the chances that others will want to become involved with or support your effort too. Leaders are generally good at reading the proverbial tea leaves, knowing a winning proposition when they see one, so success breeds success.
7. **Follow-through**: see it through until it's done. Align team member's goals and measurement objectives to their role in driving success of the initiative. Where necessary, such as for a significant corporate restructuring initiative, you may need to hire, develop, and promote people based on how well they embrace the change. Apply the Plan-Do-Check-Act methodology (described in Chapter 12) to hone your implementation approach, using short term accomplishments to leverage long term wins. In that fashion you can tackle the harder stuff like structural, policy, and system changes using early momentum.
8. **Success**: celebrate the victory. Communicate how the new state makes the organization and individuals therein more successful. Document lessons learned for future efforts. Where possible provide increased opportunities, responsibility, or recognition to those who were instrumental in making it happen. This helps create and sustain a culture of exploration and innovation.

Tackling what appears to be an insurmountable challenge is tough, but with the right vision, process, and buy-in, few things cannot be done. While your credibility may be on the line each time you take the risk, being seen as the "go to" guy or gal for resolving the truly tough problems can be a very good thing. In business it's a career-maker. In life it's a source of strength, confidence, and pride.

Follow the eight step process. Own it, hone it, and make it your own. With forethought and resolve you can be that leader who overcomes difficulties no one else knows how to undertake, inspiring others to greater heights as well.

Tackling Insurmountable Challenges

Sensei, Mentor, Leader, Coach Tip:

> No matter how well respected you are, if a challenge is seen as insurmountable no one will listen to your plans for resolving it. When faced with dire predicaments honestly acknowledge the obstacles and lay out a credible vision for success.

Action:

Don't be afraid to tackle the hard issues, but simultaneously don't feel obliged to shoulder the burden all by yourself. Whenever possible, pull stakeholders into the problem resolution process. Not only are those closest to the work intimately familiar with the factors involved, but they tend to have the most skin in the game when it comes to making things better. When you gather insight from these experts, polish it with your experience, and craft a realistic vision you will assure your best shot at success.

Give it a try. Find a systemic problem, some nagging challenge that you or members of your team have been complaining about or irritated by, and solve it. It doesn't have to be a monumental undertaking, just something meaningful enough that it's worth the effort such as streamlining an administrative burden or clarifying a confusing policy. That's the heart of continuous improvement, a never-ending endeavor to expose and eliminate root causes of problems.

Resolving a longtime thorn in your side can be the proverbial two bird/one stone victory; it puts the process to work, removes a hassle, and lets you experience how tackling the seemingly impossible can be done via the process of driving urgency, creating coalition, sharing a compelling vision, achieving buy-in, empowering people to develop solutions, making progress, following through, and reaching success. In this fashion you gain confidence, experience, and credibility.

Sensei, Mentor, Teacher, Coach – Little Life Secret:

> Most new leaders hope to make an immediate difference yet rushing headlong into change rarely has the desired effect. Strive to take the long view and cut yourself some slack. It takes time to understand challenges and opportunities, engage stakeholders, and forge coalitions before you can put viable plans in place let alone carry them through to fruition.

9

THE TURNING POINT

Making the Most of a Watershed Moment

"Luck is what happens when preparation meets opportunity."
Seneca[25]

There are a plethora of paradigms by which folks perceive the world, yet two are particularly useful when it comes to understanding success and how to go about achieving it—the Lucky Paradigm and the Effort Paradigm. Luck is oftentimes a lazy person's way of explaining achievements. It is a way to rationalize an internal lack of effort and project it onto other people's circumstances.

If a lazy person looks at another who has what he or she desires, say a boat, the person who owns the boat is "lucky." The projection of luck as the sole driving factor discounts all the hard work the other person had to undertake in order to acquire his or her resources. Look at the flow of illogical reasoning that takes place with this worldview:

Lucky Paradigm	Effort Paradigm
▫ You're lucky to have a boat	▫ I scrimped and saved for years to afford it
▫ I never get a break	▫ I made the most of my opportunities
▫ You have a good job so you could afford it	▫ I proved myself and earned the position
▫ You went to a prestigious university	▫ Good grades and test scores got me in
▫ Teachers liked you so you got good grades	▫ I studied hard and turned in my work on time
▫ My high school wasn't as good as yours	▫ I got out of school what I put into it

Arguing with a person who lives in the lucky paradigm is pointless.

You're not going to change their mind; such things must be driven from within (see Chapter 4, Flawed Thinking, for strategies on how to go about doing that). Nevertheless, understanding this perspective can be useful, particularly when taken in contrast of those who make their own luck. Effort paradigm people understand that turning points are opportunities they can create, influence, and take advantage of, not random acts of the universe.

A single point of failure is a concept that comes from manufacturing processes. It is a lynchpin in the system that, if it breaks, will grind production to a halt. The concept can be generalized to mean anything that stops your plans from moving forward. Lucky Paradigm people tend to give up when they encounter these points of failure. They stop and chalk the loss of momentum up to… well, luck, something outside their control. They are resigned to their fate.

While there may be one or more points of failure in any system, there really is no single point of success. It virtually always takes more than one thing to accomplish your objectives. What you need to look for and exploit are turning points. A turning point is a time where a decisive change has happened, usually for the better.

It takes practice and experience to know when you are seeing a turning point because they are most often recognized in retrospect. When the proverbial seas have calmed it is possible to look back over a series of events and point to the moment, or cluster of moments, where something significant occurred and label that the turning point. Take the American Civil War (1861 – 1865), for example. Historians widely consider the turning point in that conflict the Battle of Gettysburg Pennsylvania which took place from July 1st through 3rd, 1863. That period was the bloodiest battle of the entire war, a decisive victory by Union troops over the Confederate forces' greatest military leader, General Robert E. Lee.

While that battle was monumental, many historians point to a combination of events that collectively served as the turning points throughout the Civil War. One of those events may well have been the death of Lt. Gen. Stonewall Jackson following a friendly fire accident where he was hit by a bullet fired by a soldier under his own command. Jackson was loved not only by his men, but also by his commander. Upon receiving news of the incident General Lee lamented, "Jackson has lost his left arm, but I have lost my right." Jackson had been racking up one victory after another so it was reasonable to expect that if he had survived the forces under his command could have won critical battles setting the table for a possible Confederate victory at Gettysburg, which in turn would have shifted the tide of war in the Confederacy's direction.

While turning points are not always easy to discern, adopting a mindset of looking for opportunities rather than focusing on problems makes a tremendous difference. Quitting, railing against fate, and accomplishing nothing is easy. It's also stupid. Smart, directed efforts that allow you to take advantage of opportunities as they present themselves make all the difference in the outcome of events.

The next time you feel that you are in a situation that has no options, it is likely that your emotions and preconceived notions are in charge. In this mindset you will be unable to identify let alone leverage a turning point. We suggest that you take a moment, don't speak, and think about why you are having the emotion. Are you angry, frustrated?

Does the frustration, as an example, well up from the fact that you have explained something several times and the person has failed to complete the task correctly? That frustration is a block; it keeps you from achieving your objective. Your goal is not to indulge in the selfish emotion of frustration, but rather to focus on the goal you are trying to reach.

Any time you try to teach others, this frustration can come in spades. As an example we suggest breaking down the process and making it even simpler than it was before (a method which we describe in detail in Chapter 10, Break it Down, Build it Up). Focus on the goal, get the performance, and move forward. The best teachers make the assumption that failure to communicate is their problem and not the student's inherent lack of intelligence or initiative. Sound upside-down, kind of crazy? Look at it this way, adopting that mindset forces the educator to find creative ways of conveying the materials, which in turn makes him or her a better teacher.

Years ago while teaching a kids' karate class, Wilder was unable to get the students to pick their knees up high enough to throw a proper front kick. Repeated explanations, examples and repetitions were not getting results. The task was simple, lifting the knee, yet the kids failed to do it every time. It was so bad, in fact, that Wilder got it into his head that the class was refusing to lift their knees. Turning the idea that their inability to get their knees high enough to perform the technique was actually a premeditated, militant act on their part as a group to frustrate Wilder, he took it personally. Nevertheless, he really wanted to solve the problem so he sought out the help of another martial arts instructor who had many more years of teaching under his belt and asked about the situation.

This instructor made it clear. "What, you think they have secret meetings to plan out ways to mess with you?" was the gist of his reply. He also pointed out that such thinking was about Wilder's ego and not about the students, completely backwards. He further pointed out that good teachers reach their students where they are. His next tip was, "They're kids, so make it a game." Wilder did. Guess what, it worked.

Kane learned a similar trick from the associate dean he worked for at Renton Technical College. At first he lacked patience, struggling with how slowly certain students learned, but following her suggestion he began all new class sessions by telling his pupils, "If you don't get it, it's my fault." Stating it aloud forced him to adopt a much better mindset. No matter how frustrated he might become, his integrity was wrapped in finding alternate explanations that would resonate.

He then went on to encourage them to let him know whenever they did not understand the materials because, "If you don't ask the question, however, then it's your fault. The only 'stupid question' is the one you don't ask..." This approach made it easier for students to ask questions, even ones that risked exposing their ostensible naiveté, in order to better understand the curriculum and ultimately helped him receive student accolades for communicating effectively, demonstrating patience, and fostering a positive learning environment.

Sensei, Mentor, Teacher, Coach Tip:

> Viewing the world through an Effort Paradigm positions you to create your own luck. Don't stop and admire or become mired in the chaos. Your choice of mental model makes all the difference. Look to challenges as opportunities, strive to identify turning points, and exploit them to achieve success.

Action:

When you see what you consider a turning point it is important to seize the moment in a positive way. This is a critical attribute of competent military leaders. In war, success or failure often hinges on the ability to identify and exploit opportunities in a timely manner, just as it does in business, team sports, or martial arts competitions. Take some time to look up a few historical battles as a way to gain this perspective. We suggest:

- **The Battle of Cannae**: in 216 BC where the Carthaginian forces lead by Hannibal Barca killed 48,000 Romans yet only lost 8,000 of their own troops, all the while being out numbered nearly 2 to 1.
- **The Battle of Salamis**: in 480 BC this was the lessor-known second phase of the famous battle of Thermopylae where 300 Spartans held off the might of the entire Persian army. The Greek fleet drew the Persians into the Straits of Salamis and soundly defeated the superior Persian forces.
- **The Winter War**: in 1939 the outnumbered Finnish army defeated the invading Soviet forces by using geography, weather, and looting of dead Soviet soldiers for ammunition.

Not a history buff? If you are a sports fan, watch your favorite team and as the game unfolds see if you can find the turning point, the moment when victory is becoming imminent. It's often easier to recognize in the stadium than it is on TV, but there's a pretty clear ebb and flow to most games. You can see this reflected in the players' body language on the field as well as along the sidelines, in the dugout, or on the bench.

Looking at history or somebody else's sports team is one thing, but when it applies to your own life or organization turning points can be harder to see. If you are struggling, look to yourself first. Is your mindset getting in the way? Is your head in a place where you can get an objective appraisal? Is reliance on the "same old same old" limiting your perspective? Have you engaged the right people, explored enough options, and made a concerted effort to move forward?

If it seems like you are doing all the right things, seeking out turning points, and thinking beyond the obvious (see Chapter 5 for more information), yet your best effort is still not working, it may be time to put things on hold for a while. Temporarily focusing on another problem, project, or task can give you the clear-headedness necessary to see a different solution for your original challenge. Sometimes this takes a few hours, but oftentimes it can take days. Don't get discouraged. While you are consciously focusing on other things, your subconscious mind is still gnawing away at the original problem you were unable to resolve.

Success is invariably a cumulative action. You build a plan, implement, and course-correct as necessary to see it carried through (as we describe in detail when we discuss the Plan-Do-Check-Act cycle in Chapter 12). For Effort Paradigm people this is self-evident, yet when caught up in the moment we sometimes need to remind ourselves that it's a process. Giving up is not an option. Don't forget that Colonel Sanders was rejected 1,009 times before he was finally able to sell his recipe that launched Kentucky Fried Chicken. If at first you don't succeed… well, you know the rest.

The Turning Point

Sensei, Mentor, Teacher, Coach – Little Life Secret:

> The old adage, "Let me sleep on it" has real merit. Taking a fresh look at a tough situation when you are in a relaxed state changes the equation, and sleeping is about as relaxed as you can get. Further it allows the sub-conscience to work on the issue in an unobstructed manner. Rene Descartes related that the innovations for his new philosophy, The Scientific Method, came to him in a dream. Pretty powerful stuff to have slept on…

10

BREAK IT DOWN, BUILD IT UP

The Big Bad Chunk and the Three Little Chunks

"You can break that big plan into small steps and take the first step right away."
Indira Gandhi[26]

Sensei, mentors, educators, and coaches do a lot of teaching. Sometimes that's relatively easy as these folks tend to be masters of their subjects and know a multitude of ways to explain their materials, but as you've no doubt experienced oftentimes it's really tough. Part of the challenge depends on the audience.

While teaching children can be a lot like filling empty vessels with facts and ideas there is little context to leverage, so you need to start slow, explain the fundamentals, and work your way up toward the more complicated stuff. Adults have more context and experience, yet concepts can no longer simply be poured in. New ideas must be fitted into what is already there which brings up a host of additional complications, especially if what they think they know is wrong.

Complex concepts or techniques are best taught as a series of simple principles or movements that, once mastered, can be reintegrated into a whole. We call that "chunking." Like chapters in a book, it segments complicated materials into digestible components. For youthful learners the "bites" may need to be smaller, yet this process can help you succeed no matter what audience you are addressing.

Chunking works just as well for conveying knowledge as it does for physical skills, but we'll use a simple karate technique to demonstrate the concept. Let's say you want to teach a new student a front kick. Your goal is to have the student understand and execute the basics successfully. And, since success breeds success, you want him or her to learn to apply the application as quickly as possible.

Over Chunk: explain the context

We begin with an "over chunk," that is setting the stage by explaining context. For certain learning styles it is vital to understand the big picture before any progress can be made, whereas for others it is not required but virtually always helpful (so long as you don't get overly longwinded about it and lose folks' interest). With physical skills such as the front kick this is often done by explaining as well as demonstrating, as this approach plays to both visual and auditory learners. Afterward students get to practice and receive reinforcement, playing to the kinesthetic as well. This combination tends to sink in better than merely explaining alone since it accommodates all three major learning styles. Here is an example:

> "The front kick is used to strike at a person in front of you. It is a fast kick, a strong kick and one of the 'go to' fundamentals of karate. We will do this kick a lot in our training because it is very useful in tournaments and on the street."

This talk orients the student by conveying the key elements. And it is underscores the importance of what they are about to learn.

1. **Chunk One:** beginning correctly

Beginning correctly takes forethought. As the instructor you are solely responsible for the quality of the education. Further, beginning correctly sets your student or mentee up for success. Without this you are in for a lot of angst and frustration. A challenge is that if you are really good at something, especially where knowledge or skills came naturally, you may have trouble knowing why. This is the reason that so many sports superstars are lousy teachers; they cannot articulate what made them so good in ways that others can grasp and emulate. Spend time thinking about the fundamental underpinnings necessary to make whatever you are trying to teach work so that you can logically and adroitly explain it to someone who may have a harder time latching onto the concept than you did.

> *"Are you right handed? It is likely that if you are right handed you are also right footed, so let's begin by standing like this with your dominant leg back. We'll kick with that foot."*

It is easier for most people to kick when they wind-up like a baseball pitcher, as they are able to use momentum in lieu of fine muscle control which takes trained effort. By performing the technique with their dominant leg students have an easier time maintaining their balance on their opposite foot than if they were to switch feet and attempt it the other way around. Another alternative to keep from falling over is to have the trainee hold onto a chair or rail. The specific example doesn't really matter all that much; setting the student up for success, on the other hand, is everything.

2. **Chunk Two:** sequential order

Starting at the beginning of the processes is pretty obvious, but be thoughtful about the order so that basic actions can be drilled, mastered, and stacked together to become more complex and powerful. Like climbing a mountain there is often more than one way to reach the summit, so in order to achieve your end goal think about the method that is most efficient from the learner's perspective then tailor your instruction to meet your audience's level of experience and ability to understand.

> *"All kicks begin with a knee lift. The process is to lift the knee up, strike outward forcefully, and then pull your leg back as quickly as possible. We'll just do the first movement for now. Lift your foot off of the floor and bring your knee up to waist height like this. If you bend your support leg slightly it will help you balance. Now you try it. Good. We don't spend a lot of time lifting our knees up to our waist on a daily basis, so it's an unnatural movement but you looked pretty good. Now, a little higher. The higher you lift your*

knee, the higher you can kick. Let me turn sideways and show you again…"

Sequential order is based on two initial actions that we will begin to stack upon. For physical skills be sure to explain, demonstrate, and let the student practice. If the foundation is solid and the order of actions is logical, the student can quickly add more and more layers onto the beginning point.

3. **Chunk Three:** stacking

Stacking comes after the initial move is repeated and done in a manner that is satisfactory. Now we add one more movement at a time. In our kicking example, the next step is thrusting the lower leg outward. To avoid falling down, the student must be able to balance on one leg, lift their knee to waist height, and then extend their foot outward toward a target. As you can see, each of these items utilizes the student's muscles differently for control and balance, yet if taught in the right sequence the movements are easily mastered.

> *"Excellent! That's pretty good for a first time out. Now when your knee reaches waist height that is the trigger to snap your lower leg outward. Pull your toes back so that you are aiming with the ball of your foot. It hurts to hit something solid with your bare toes. Knee up, strike outward. Let's give it a try..."*

Stacking can have as many additions as needed. We like to think of these as data points. Just like making a graph, without the specific data points whatever is being taught will fail. Imagine trying to do a front kick by lifting your knee without thrusting the lower leg forward. It not a front kick any more, it is a knee strike. Lifting your knee and kicking outward without continuing through the progression by pulling your leg back and setting your foot down is ineffectual (and silly looking). As you can see, each data point is essential. When done in the correct sequential order the data begins to flow naturally which is why stacking is so successful at bringing incremental growth to the task.

This example probably seems overly simplistic, but for someone who has never set foot inside a *dojo* the simple task of kicking properly can be daunting. Providing too much information at once is overwhelming, a common challenge in little league sports. Players may be inclined to give up because leaning the new task is too hard, too confusing, yet all that is necessary is a little patience and forethought on the coaches' part. Chunking virtually any type of new knowledge into fundamental components allows you to communicate complex ideas simply and efficiently.

While we used a karate example, the same thing works for swinging a bat, throwing a football, or learning algebra. It applies to business projects and programs too. Look at the end goal, break it down into component parts, and work backwards from success criteria, due dates, and the like to map out all the steps necessary to get there. Assure that the plan covers your project's scope, objectives, assumptions, risks, resources, and organization. Oftentimes this is done via a work breakdown structure and integrated schedule, though that level of diligence is not always warranted. Once the plan has been adequately chunked, you can move forward to acquire resources, build skills where necessary, and assemble all the component pieces in a logical construct that assures you will accomplish the work on time.

No matter what the endeavor, by breaking component tasks into digestible pieces and explaining each in a logical sequential order you can achieve success far quicker than you may have thought possible.

Sensei, Mentor, Teacher, Coach Tip:

> As a policy we suggest not correcting more than three things during any single training session. Even for highly skilled individuals too much information can be overwhelming. It is important to recognize what may have already have been communicated by another instructor or coach as well. If the person has already been getting correction, make an effort to not add new materials until they are capable of processing them. Try to support what may have already been taught by others unless it is fundamentally flawed too; there is more than one "right" way to accomplish many tasks.

Action:

Here is how to chunk using a piece of paper and pencil: Turn the paper landscape on your desk. Now draw an arch from left to right, like a rainbow. Write on this arch the goal that you wish to accomplish. In our example it was, "Teach students how to perform a front kick." Next create three boxes underneath the arch. These are your three chunks. If in filling in the boxes you discover that you've jumped to too high a level, segment each chunk into three underlying components. Once you have the appropriate level of detail, take your completed work to the instructional moment. You can even go so far as taping it on the wall if needed. Follow it and see just how smooth your instruction becomes. It is a great presentation technique too.

For highly complex, long-term, or challenging projects or programs you will want to take things to the next level, utilizing project management best practices (oftentimes led by a trained and certified professional). This process analyzes requirements and chunks tasks into manageable components by creating plans for project, resource, financial, quality, risk, and change management, procurement, governance, communication, and the like. That's far too complex to go into here, volumes of work are written on that subject alone, but be aware of organizations that can help such as The Project Management Institute (www.pmi.org) or online resources such as the Project Management Hut (www.pmhut.com).

Sensei, Mentor, Teacher, Coach – Little Life Secret:

> Rather than asking about what has already been taught, have new students, mentees, or athletes explain prerequisites you think they should know to someone else. Having to verbalize what a person has learned is a great way to drive the instruction deeper. One of the reasons that most advanced martial arts students are obliged to teach as a part of fulfilling the requirements necessary to earn their black belt is that the process of explaining things to others increases retention and understanding.

11

THREEFOLD MISSION STATEMENT

Three Steps to Calibrating Your Internal Compass

"An artist is not paid for his labor but for his vision."
James Whistler[27]

People often confuse labor with vision. They might say, "I don't know why that executive gets paid five million dollars when a factory worker only gets $17.50 an hour." We are not here to engage in the political argument, let others chew that fat. The mere fact you have picked up this book means that you are different. You have a vision.

Nicola Tesla was a man of vision as well. He created the induction motor, the remote controlled vehicle, radio, and more. Even though he died in 1943, Tesla is personally responsible for the core of much of our modern technology today, yet Tesla worked as a simple laborer when he landed in the United States after leaving Serbia. Nevertheless, he was not destined to dig ditches any more than Einstein was destined to be a mere patent clerk. There's nothing wrong with using your hands and the sweat of your brow to make a living, but becoming an ordinary laborer is not what most folks yearn to be.

Tesla and Einstein were extraordinary; they both aspired to greater things. But, those two men lived in a different time, not as cluttered and not nearly as noisy as the world we have today. If you want to be like them, you need a tool, a method of building your focus. That's where a vision statement comes in.

A vision statement is a vivid description of a desired outcome that inspires and energizes. It paints a mental picture of success in clear and compelling terms. It could be as lofty as a vision for your ideal life or something modest as the outcome of a game plan or work project. Consequently you will undoubtedly have several vision statements, using them for a variety of different purposes.

One of the simplest yet most profound ways to do this is with a vision board, a pictorial representation of your aspirations. For many, this personal vision board is the place to start.

Creating a Vision Board:

One effective technique you can use is the cut-and-paste method, seeking out pictures that create a collage representing where you want to be at some critical juncture in your life. It is better to do that with scissors and glue than to use your computer. Done this way, a vision board may sound like a child's kindergarten project. In some ways it is, yet the process of putting a vision board together is actually a way to reach a deeper place. You see the human mind doesn't actually think in words, it uses pictures and symbols. If we talk to you about a tree, you don't think of the letters "T-R-E-E," you think of an image, a representation of a tree. Do not dismiss the power of symbols as you begin the process of building your vision.

Oftentimes the pictures you select will represent a higher level within the strata you are in. An instance of this might be placing a photo of a Lamborghini Countach on your vision board when you are currently driving a ratty "econobox" with month old French fries and dirty gym socks under the back seat.

A vision board collage is fine, the physical act of creating one helps unify your vision and point your thought process toward the steps necessary for getting there. But, you need to make it real. For example, if you were able to reach the point in your life where you actually did own that shiny new Lamborghini Countach, is it likely that you would still have smelly old French fries under your fine leather seats? "Not a chance!" you'd probably say, right? But, think carefully on that. If your current car is unwashed and cluttered with junk, the direction of your internal compass has not changed. You are still in an econobox mindset. An external goal may have been posted on the board, but you have not built a mindset that can take you where you want to go.

The expression "dress for the job you want, not the job you have" comes into play here. We know it sounds trite, but there is truth in that statement. Garish attire, wrinkled suits, or stained uniforms communicate your internal world to others. For example, responding to popular yet unappealing "hip-hop" fashion of the time (e.g., do-rags, oversized jewelry, baggy jeans), the National Basketball Association became the first professional sports league in the United States to implement a mandatory dress code for its players in 2005. Commissioner David Stern insisted that all players dress in conservative business attire when arriving at games, sitting on the bench while injured, leaving stadiums, or conducting official business on behalf of the NBA such as giving interviews or putting on charity events.

As a teacher, mentor, or coach it is important that you look at your vision board, be it a physical manifestation or merely an aspiration in your head. Continuing the Lamborghini example, the Countach demonstrates wealth, power, and virility. It can create envy or desire in others as well. It will likely be perceived as pretentious, impractical, and over-the-top too. Think about what each item on your board represents. Does it lead you toward a future of who and what you truly want to be?

So, set this book down and build your vision board. Seriously, do it now.

Warning: do not read ahead before making your vision board because it will diminish the value of this exercise. Once you're done with the drill, you get to read the following section to interpret your results. To help protect you fast readers, the next set of instructions are written in a simple code to slow you down. Every other word is reversed:

Read ruoy vision draob from tfel to thgir now. Eht items no the tfel side fo the draob tend ot represent eht items that are ni the tsap of ruoy life. Eht middle si the tneserp and eht far thgir is tahw you era holding rof the erutuf.

This is your subconscious unmasked. Now you have a better idea of what you think and how it matches up to what your mind says about itself in the dark places of your skull.

Creating a Personal Mission Statement:

A vision board is a useful place to start, but for most people it is not enough. If you find yourself drifting, out of sorts, or disgruntled it is oftentimes a result of straying from the essence of who you or what you want to be at your core. Putting your values in writing and referring back to them from time to time helps you stay centered. A great way to do that is with a personal mission statement. This declaration should answer three vital questions:

1. What is my life about (purpose)?
2. What do I stand for (values)?
3. What actions will I take (to manifest my purpose and values)?

1. **What is my life about** (purpose)?

Years ago Wilder worked in downtown Seattle. Every morning he would ride the elevator in the Federal Building. The ride up was often full of empty talk. "It's a Monday." "Yup, it's a Monday." That sort of thing...

One morning a guy piped up with a non sequitur, breaking the silence, "Eighteen months, four days." A pause and somebody asked, "What is eighteen months, four days?" He responded, "That is how long until I retire." The same guy asked, "Then what are you going to do?" Moving his eyes down from the blinking floor indicator above the door, he replied, "Fish."

Fishing is fun, but it's hardly a purpose for living. A purpose in life should be much bigger, fuller, juicier, and more vibrant than what that poor schlub in the elevator espoused. The first part of answering this question is to search your soul to find what really spikes your life, brings the pop. Then ask yourself the question, why does this pop for me and how can I use this help others.

That poor schlub who just wanted to fish, it's a safe bet that fishing eventually lost its luster. The reason is simple, that guy's choice was selfish. Selfish is shallow. Had they talked Wilder might have suggested donating a few days a month to help less fortunate folks learn to enjoy fishing. Sharing the joy makes it sustainable because it grows.

So, what is your life's purpose? Write it down. Don't worry about polish, just get thoughts on paper. You'll get a chance to wordsmith as much as you need to after you have completed the next two steps.

My life's purpose is: _____

_____

_____

2. What do I stand for (values)?

Values describe your core as a human being, a pretty profound subject. For many it is tough to articulate, but since a values statement cuts to who you are it should not be. The statement should not be long either; oftentimes a word or two will suffice, but the challenge is that it is much tougher for most folks to come up with that one perfect word or sentence than it is for them to write several hundred that are somewhere in the ballpark. Don't sweat it, there's a process:

- Grab a pen and a sheet of paper and start listing what you find important in life. You could type, but many find that the physical act of writing longhand helps them coalesce their thoughts in a more artistic way, with a little more feeling.
- Do not limit the subjects. It can be faith, family, friends, work, a vocation, gardening, sports, education, or virtually anything else… there is no limit.
- Importantly, don't think too hard. Just do it. That's one of the reasons for choosing a pen instead of a pencil, you can't erase.
- Use a timer. Give yourself only thirty seconds to complete the assignment, maybe a minute or two if you're a slow writer. For best success, it needs to be quick. You want a stream of consciousness and not a doctoral thesis.

Like your life's purpose, you may be tempted to edit and update what you have just written but that's premature. All you need at the moment is the brainstormed list you just created. After the next step you will pull things together and refine as much as necessary.

My values are: _____

_____

_____

3. What actions will I take?

Now that you are able to articulate your purpose and values it is time to do something with it. How do you make it real? What is the vehicle you can latch onto to exploit the flow of your purpose? Map out the things you plan to do or change near term and long term in order to turn your personal mission statement into a reality. This could take a while. Start by drawing a line down the middle of a piece of paper. Label one side "near term" and the other side "long term," and then start writing. Once again a stream of consciousness is all you need for now. Refinement comes next.

Actions I will take:

Near Term	Long Term

Pulling it all together:

Armed with your purpose, values, and actions, it's time to write things down in a more coherent manner. The key is to hurt your head on it, really think things through, put it in writing, and tweak it as much as you like to get it "right." Once complete, be sure to look back on it frequently. This time you are better off using a computer so that it's easier to edit and refine your work.

There is no right or wrong way to craft your personal mission statement. It is, after all, personal. It should have whatever level of detail you feel is most appropriate to act as your guide. We have included an example below. Note values, purpose, and actions in these statements:

- Deeply enjoy life, living, and the wonders of creation. Harmoniously balance professional, social, and family commitments.
- Act bravely, courteously, and honorably. Treat everyone with dignity, fairness, trust, and respect to ensure that I am worthy of such consideration from others. Be humble to graciously accept constructive feedback, but do not abide personal attacks.
- Learn constantly. Take responsibility for accomplishments and failures alike, for failure is merely an opportunity to learn. Challenge myself to forever try new things, seek new knowledge, gain new understanding, and ultimately achieve true wisdom.
- Cherish relationships. Make daily deposits in the emotional bank accounts of those close to me. Build bridges through keeping trust, honoring commitments, showing concern, and demonstrating friendship.
- Be a good role model. Demonstrate the virtues of courtesy, honesty, integrity, and service, so that my son will know that chivalry and honor have meaning in everyday life. Be someone my son will be proud to call father and my wife will be proud to call husband.
- Try to give something back. Support social, community, and religious institutions, giving of my time and resources as they are needed.

To be of any use, your personal mission statement needs to come from the heart, not just the head. Much like the collage you built earlier, it should paint a vivid vision of how you wish to live your life, what you want to aspire to, only with words rather than pictures this time. Once it's polished to your satisfaction print it out.

Keep your personal mission statement in front of you and make it real. When you use it to chart the course of your life you will find that you become more excited to get up in the morning, more productive throughout the day, and generally happier at all times.

A personal mission statement can be a tremendously valuable guide, yet businesses, schools, and teams need the same thing as well. In fact, in many ways it is even more important for organizations where a well-written mission and vision can get everyone on the same page with minimal effort.

Think about how tough it would be on players if the offensive coordinator, position coaches, and head coach weren't all on the same page. Sound unlikely? Unfortunately not so much, even on fundamentals... For instance, like most timing patterns the hitch route in American football is designed to go to a pre-determined location on the field so that when the receiver turns the ball is already on its way from the quarterback, hence harder to defend against. As a sideline reporter Kane has overheard heated arguments amongst the coaching staff of more than one high school varsity football team about whether the hitch route should be based on the number of steps or number of yards the receiver should run before turning around and coming back for the ball.

This phenomenon is nothing new. When Kane took an administration, organizational theory and design class in college his professor described businesses as gigantic cardboard boxes. To continue the analogy if you were to put the best engineer, the best marketer, the best mechanic, the best finance person, and so on, all the essential roles, into the box and tell them to move it, they will. The challenge is that they are likely to start pushing on different walls. Not only does the box not go anywhere, but this dysfunction is really hard on the box.

Mission and vision statements supported by clear objectives help align actions, getting everyone pushing on the same wall of the metaphorical box. It's not easy, square objects don't roll particularly well, but the box will begin to move. It will bulge, bend, and become a bit misshapen along the way, but once it picks up steam the box will move pretty effectively so long as everyone keeps pushing on the same wall.

So, how do you do this? Building a personal mission statement is tough enough, but at least you're the only person doing the work and you have a process for accomplishing it. It can be far more challenging for leaders of organizations to reach consensus necessary to form a collective vision and mission because everyone with a vote has to agree. We have found in these situations that it helps to start with a clarity exercise to align thoughts and identify key words. Armed with this "homework," leaders can have a robust discussion about their organization. Here's how it works…

Clarity Exercise:

Creating alignment is essential to building and maintaining a healthy organization, be it a small business, large corporation, department, or sports team. Inconsistencies can confuse and dishearten stakeholders. There are six critical questions that need to be answered to assure that everyone is on the same page. Have the leadership team complete this exercise before you meet to work on the organization's mission and vision.

Answer each of the questions below **in three sentences or less**, enough information to spark conversation but not so much folks get locked into a certain way of thinking due to pride of authorship. These questions have been adapted from www.mindtools.com, which is a fantastic resource for leaders in any profession, well worth checking out if you are not already familiar with it.

1. **Why does our organization exist?** *The answer to this question will yield a core purpose, the fundamental reason the organization is in business. This foundation supports development of the mission statement.*
2. **How do we behave?** *This question examines behaviors and values required for success. These values support development of the vision statement.*
3. **What do we do?** *This answer provides a simple, direct explanation of the organization. It is a vital underpinning for the mission statement.*
4. **How will we succeed?** *This question requires team members to develop the foundation for a strategy. Typically this will lead to goals and objectives, but it could support either the mission or vision depending on how folks respond to the question.*
5. **What is most important right now?** *The answer to this question is the establishment of a unifying thematic goal and*

action plan. Once again it supports development of tactics later on, but it also helps the team craft a vision statement.
6. **Who must do what?** *This question addresses roles and responsibilities. It supports creation of the vision statement.*

Compile responses from the leadership team and use tagcloud.com or a similar method of identifying common themes and thoughts to facilitate discussion. Tagcloud works by identifying key words and displaying them in larger or smaller text depending on how many times they came up during the clarity exercise responses. In this fashion you get a report that shows areas of agreement, at least at a cursory level, without needing to delve into the details of what any specific individual has written. This lets leaders collectively coalesce their thoughts, spurring meaningful dialogue with minimal contention.

The output might look something like this:

> maintain team **value** achieve applications **business**
>
> company **competitive** deliver design employees
>
> enable content world class **integrated** manage
>
> **people** products **reliable** scalable **secure**
>
> technology standards customers outcomes **information**
>
> improvements **partner** empowered service

As you can see by this example it is easy to identify common themes, in this instance integrated, reliable, secure information that adds value for the business. Armed with the results of this exercise, you are ready to have robust discussions in which you can develop your organization's mission and vision statements. It's not the answers of this clarity exercise that matter as much as the discussions that take place afterward.

The more aligned your thought process and expectations, the easier it will be to collectively chart the organization's future. Mission should come first, followed by vision. Later on specific goals and objectives will be needed to assure implementation, especially in large organizations. We have already talked about SMART goal setting in Chapter 6, so we'll just focus on creating the mission and vision statements here.

Creating an Organizational Mission Statement:

A mission statement defines the organization's purpose and primary objectives. Its function is internal, to define and communicate key measures of success. While it might be shared outside, the prime audience is the leadership team, employees, and stakeholders within the organization.

To create your mission statement, first identify your organization's "winning idea." Next identify the key measures of your success. Make sure you choose only the most important measures and not too many. Combine your winning idea and success criteria into a tangible and measurable goal. Refine the words until you have a concise and precise statement of your mission, which expresses your ideas, measures and desired results.

It often takes a lot of refinement and wordsmithing to get it "just right" but it is virtually always worth the effort. The end result does not have to be complicated or lengthy. Try to keep it pithy. An example of an extremely well-written mission statement comes from Starbucks:

> *"Our mission: To inspire and nurture the human spirit—one person, one cup and one neighborhood at a time."*

You can feel the essence of Starbucks in those words, right? And read them on all their coffee cups. Once the mission has been agreed upon and documented, move on to develop the vision statement.

Creating an Organizational Vision Statement:

Vision statements define the organization's purpose in terms of guiding principles, values and beliefs. For employees, it gives direction about how they are expected to behave and inspires them to give their best. Shared with customers and suppliers, it shapes their understanding of why they should want to work with you. Done right this can be really powerful stuff.

To create a vision statement, begin by identifying what you, your customers, and other stakeholders will value most about how your organization will achieve its mission. Distill these into the values that your organization has or should have. An example of a well-written vision statement comes from United Parcel Service (UPS):

- **Integrity**: it is the core of who we are and all we do
- **Teamwork**: determined people working together can accomplish anything
- **Service**: serving the needs of our customers and communities is central to our success
- **Quality and efficiency**: we remain constructively dissatisfied in our pursuit of excellence
- **Safety**: the well-being of our people, business partners, and the public is of utmost importance
- **Sustainability**: long-term prosperity requires our continued commitment to environmental stewardship and social responsibility
- **Innovation**: creativity and change are essential to growth

Once you have solid drafts, combine your mission and vision onto one page and polish the words until you have a statement inspiring enough to energize and motivate people inside and outside your organization. If it takes more than a single page it's too long; no one will read or remember it. Keep this document in front of you, refer back to it repeatedly, and don't let it get stale if the fundamentals of your organization or business environment change (if done right it will weather the ages without needing updating, but it pays to check back every year or two to be certain).

Many companies post their mission and vision statements in all their conference rooms, break rooms, and offices as well as on their website. Here's an example from Southwest Airlines:

| We operate with a Warrior Spirit, a Servant's Heart, and a Fun-LUVing Attitude | The mission of Southwest Airlines is dedication to the highest quality of Customer Service delivered with a sense of warmth, friendliness, individual pride, and Company Spirit.

To Our Employees:
We are committed to provide our Employees a stable work environment with equal opportunity for learning and personal growth. Creativity and innovation are encouraged for improving the effectiveness of Southwest Airlines. Above all, Employees will be provided the same concern, respect, and caring attitude within the organization that they are expected to share externally with every Southwest Customer.

To Our Communities:
Our goal is to be the hometown airline of every community we serve, and because those communities sustain and nurture us with their support and loyalty, it is vital that we, as individuals and in groups, embrace each community with the SOUTHWEST SPIRIT of involvement, service, and caring to make those communities better places to live and work.

To Our Planet:
We strive to be a good environmental steward across our system in all of our hometowns, and one component of our stewardship is efficiency, which, by its very nature, translates to eliminating waste and conserving resources. Using cost-effective and environmentally beneficial operating procedures (including facilities and equipment) allows us to reduce the amount of materials we use and, when combined with our ability to reuse and recycle material, preserves these environmental resources.

To Our Stakeholders:
Southwest's vision for a sustainable future is one where there will be a balance in our business model between Employees and Community, the Environment, and our Financial Viability. In order to protect our world for future generations, while meeting our commitments to our Employees, Customers, and Stakeholders, we will strive to lead our industry in innovative efficiency that conserves natural resources, maintains a creative and innovative workforce, and gives back to the communities in which we live and work. |

Threefold Mission Statement

When visible, measurable, and managed, well-written mission and vision statements can be powerful tools for driving organizational success. To really become and remain real, however, these words need to be backed up by specific goals that are used to align and document individual performance in carrying out the organization's objectives. In Chapter 6 we talk about SMART goals, which is a very good way to do that.

Sensei, Mentor, Teacher, Coach Tip:

> People seldom hit what they do not aim at. Crafting a vision and mission for yourself and your organization helps articulate the purpose, values, and actions necessary to stay on track. Take the time to lay out your plan properly, it may take a week, or may even require a couple of months, but our experience says that winging it on a daily basis or crafting a slap-dash plan that only takes moments to create is a waste of time.

Action:

If you have not already developed your threefold personal mission statement do so now. Your organization may have already enumerated its vision, mission, values, and goals too. If not, best get started.

Sensei, Mentor, Teacher, Coach – Little Life Secret:

> The shorter, more concise a plan is the more likely it is be followed. The more inclusive and verbose a statement the less useful it becomes. Statements over seventeen words begin to diminish in effectiveness, so keep it pithy.

12

PLAN – DO – CHECK – ACT

Measure Twice, Cut Once

*"The greatest waste is failure to use the abilities of people...
to learn about their frustrations and about the
contributions that they are eager to make."*
W. Edwards Deming[28]

A popular tool for managing change and improving processes is the Deming Wheel, named for its proponent W. Edwards Deming. A pioneer of lean manufacturing and continuous improvement (*kaizen* in Japanese) he invented the Plan-Do-Check-Act cycle. A ubiquitous tool in business, particularly where reliable, repeatable processes drive competitive advantage, it is not as well known to or adopted by teachers, coaches, and others who can benefit from it as well.

Here is the process:

- **Plan**: identifying and analyzing the problem
- **Do**: developing and testing a potential solution
- **Check**: measuring how effective the test solution was and analyzing whether it could be improved in any way
- **Act**: implementing the improved solution fully

As you can see, there are four phases of this process, yet it is not static. One should continuously cycle through the steps as solutions are refined, retested, re-refined and retested yet again in search of perfection. In this fashion you take a methodical approach to problem solving and solution implementation. Sometimes you can flash through the steps in rapid fashion, while other times deep thought and analysis must be applied.

If you follow these steps you set yourself up to get the highest quality, highest value solution possible for any given problem. And, importantly, you don't get so locked into how you've been doing something that you become unwilling or unable to look at better alternatives.

The process begins with a "Planning" phase in which the problem is clearly identified and understood. Potential solutions are then generated and tested on a small scale in the "Do" phase, and the outcome of this testing is evaluated during the Check phase. "Do" and "Check" phases can be iterated as many times as is necessary before the full, polished solution is implemented in the "Act" phase.

No matter how prepared we think we are for any given endeavor, things inevitably go wrong. Our best-laid plans simply will not work right every time. To paraphrase Will Rogers, when you find yourself in a hole, the first thing you want to do is stop digging. If a check shows that the plan is not working, stop. Adjust the plan accordingly and then proceed with a modification, hence the "Act" phase. Obviously when things go well the appropriate act is continuance of the original plan.

When plans go awry, as they frequently do, this P-D-C-A context allows a leader to exercise his or her creativity and flexibility to make in-course corrections without undue panic, stress, or wasted time. This builds reliable, repeatable processes that can drive and sustain competitive advantage. We'll walk through each phase in a little more detail…

Step 1: Plan

First, identify exactly what your problem is. This seems simple at first blush but oftentimes it is challenging to articulate the root cause and not launch off into solving symptoms rather than fixing the problem (as we discussed in Chapter 5, Thinking Beyond the Obvious). For example, if you are an American football coach and your ground game isn't working is the problem the running back, the quarterback, the offensive line, or something completely different? Are you taking best advantage of your player's strengths or playing against the opponent's defensive forte?

The planning process does not need to be arduous. It can be as simple as gathering your thoughts before speaking to as complex as building a long range business plan or IT application rollout strategy. The point is to clearly identify your goal and lay out concrete steps for getting there.

Step 2: Do

This phase involves generating and analyzing potential solutions. In a manufacturing context it might include small-scale pilot projects or scientific trials to vet scenarios, whereas in a martial arts instructional setting it might be a single lesson plan. In a tournament it might be a new trick you wish to try in order to defeat your opponent. The point is that it's a trial run that you're looking for, not a full blown solution.

The innovation principle of "fail early, fail often" applies here. In this manner if your proposed solution does not work out, you have not wasted too much time and effort before moving on to the next attempt. And, you don't have so much emotion invested in your original direction that you become unwilling to make a change.

Step 3: Check

In this phase, you measure how effective the initial solution has been, gathering information that could be used to make it even better. Depending on the success of your pilot, how many improvements you have been able to identify, and your overall scope you may elect to repeat the first two steps or you might launch into step four. That's the goal of the check step, a determination of whether or not you've found a solution you are willing or able to fully implement.

This process was originally designed for manufacturing processes, continuously driving better and better solutions until you have perfected the efficiency, effectiveness, and quality of the final product yet it works equally well for long term endeavors such as building a winning sports program or honing an individual competitor's skills. Through testing your strategy and tactics in multiple scenarios you can refine the underlying knowledge, skills, and abilities needed to win consistently. It helps to document scenarios and results, much as winning baseball skippers focus on statistics to know which pitchers should be used in various game settings.

Step 4: Act

The final step is where you fully implement your preferred solution. It generally does not mean that you have completed the P-D-C-A process, just that you have reached a stable plateau from which to launch your next round of improvements. The process truly never ends as perfection is rarely if ever achieved. Further, with the possible exception of certain products or services with very long lifecycles, changes in technology, regulations, business climate, and the like tend to drive the need for changes in the way you do things. This applies not only to businesses, but also to sports teams, academic institutions, and the like. The world is not a static place.

Sensei, Mentor, Teacher, Coach Tip:

> It is easy to get locked into historic solutions, the way you've always done things, especially when the old ways worked and appear to remain successful. The challenge is that while historic solutions may still work, they are oftentimes no longer the best approach. This is where the Plan-Do-Check-Act cycle can really add value. It allows you to continuously evolve by identifying suboptimal situations, testing potential solutions, course-correcting, and implementing the best possible remedies in a timely manner.

Action:

When laying out lesson plans, tackling challenging problems, or implementing long term programs identify opportunities to put the Plan-Do-Check-Act cycle into play. It is a simple yet effective approach for product development, problem solving, change management, and the like, ensuring that ideas are appropriately tested before committing to full implementation.

Plan – Do – Check – Act

There are few perfect answers. Oftentimes you will need to choose from amongst a variety of potential solutions to test using this process. While it can be intuitively obvious which one to select, there's a simple tool that can help you decide which way to go when things get a little more complicated. It's called a grid analysis.

To perform a grid analysis, create a matrix showing your various alternatives and rank them against relevant criteria such as quality, cost, cycle time, service levels, safety, morale, or whatever is appropriate. Your valuations can be as simple as a scale that runs from 1 (low) to 5 (high), though they may also include weightings that distribute scores based on the relative importance of the various criteria as needed.

Here's an example:

	Quality	Cost	Cycle Time	Service Level	Safety	Morale	Total
Option 1	5	3	3	3	3	1	18
Option 2	4	4	5	3	4	3	23
Option 3	4	5	2	3	4	4	22
Option 4	2	3	2	5	3	3	18
Option 5	2	3	4	3	4	5	21

In some cases, this matrix provides all the information you need to know in order to move forward with your plan. It's easy to overcomplicate or overanalyze such things, so keep it simple whenever possible. Nevertheless, it is crucial to understand what success truly looks like before making any decisions. There are tradeoffs in just about everything. Are you sure that you have considered all the right categories? Is cost savings more important than morale? Does quality trump cycle time? Is safety something you could ever compromise? When necessary assign relative weightings amongst the categories before you run the numbers.

Pretending for the moment that weightings don't matter in our illustration, Option 2 seems to be the best choice, the first alternative to run through the P-D-C-A cycle, followed by Option 3 if the first try doesn't work as expected. If still not satisfied with the result, you would then move on to Option 5. If none of those initial choices work out as expected you might be well served to reevaluate your plans rather than cycle through every option, though you could certainly do that as well.

Below is the analysis again, this time with weightings. To create a total score we simply multiply the rating for each category by the weighting of that category and add them up. A heavier emphasis on some attributes of the solution such as quality over others like cycle time changes the answer. Now, Option 3 is our first choice rather than Option 2.

	Quality	Cost	Cycle Time	Service Level	Safety	Morale	Total
Weight	30	10	5	20	20	15	100
Option 1	5	3	3	3	3	1	330
Option 2	4	4	5	3	4	3	370
Option 3	4	5	2	3	4	4	380
Option 4	2	3	2	5	3	3	305
Option 5	2	3	4	3	4	5	325

Use the Plan-Do-Check-Act cycle to help maintain an open mind, evaluate possible solutions to challenges as they arise, and continuously improve your organization. When selecting amongst options where an optional solution is not clear, utilize the grid analysis to help decide which choice to undertake first.

Sensei, Mentor, Teacher, Coach – Little Life Secret:

> The art of leadership is not checking off on SMART goals, the Plan-Do-Check-Act cycle, grid analysis, or any other tool on a continual basis, it is in understanding the principles and having them quietly operating in the background.

13

CROSS-POLLINATION

Leveraging the Strength of Diversity

"Diversity: the art of thinking independently together."
Malcolm Forbes[29]

Ever eat a Golden Delicious apple? The sweet, yellow colored one? The tree that grows this apple is sterile; it cannot pollinate itself, so it has to have pollen from adjacent apple trees in order to bear fruit. That process is called cross-pollination, an agricultural term that means the transfer of pollen from the anther (male cone) of one flower to the stigma (female cone) of another flower on a different plant, typically by insects, wind, and the like. The result in this instance is a large golden apple that is sweet and good to eat.

Like the apple tree, you owe it to yourself and those you influence to cross-pollinate. We are not suggesting you or your thought process is sterile, not at all, but we are suggesting that seeking information outside of your industry or area of expertise can help you generate much better solutions than doing things all by yourself or solely with those of similar backgrounds and experience. Much like Golden Delicious apples' cross-pollination makes for a highly improved experience, so does leveraging the diversity of others.

Think about it this way. As a teacher, what can a magician teach you? Put aside the magic act and look at the process. A magician needs to enwrap his or her audience in the experience. What are the attributes of this experience? Is it the clothes? The mannerisms? What about the words that are used, the diction? All these factors are used to transport spectators to a new place, a new world through illusion. What would happen if you got a book on the presentation of magic and read it? Would you find a nugget or two that you could use to better your leadership? If nothing else, would it help you become a better speaker? In all likelihood the answer is yes.

Speaking of speeches, what makes a great speaker? What can you learn from Dr. Martin Luther King when it comes to oration? On first bounce we'd say, "Speak from the heart. Don't just give information, but give your feelings too." If you want to be a proficient speaker, going out and finding the top ten keys to delivering a good speech is a nice place to start, but you are only going to learn the mechanics, not the fire. Without a love of the subject, you get no juice. A good speech is remembered by how people felt, not necessarily what was said or heard.

Kane currently works in Information Technology (IT) where he is responsible, among other things, for developing the business strategy of a $1.2B a year organization. Sounds impressive, perhaps, yet it is just one department within a major company (it's a really big company). Part of the reason he was selected for this position is that he is naturally a strategic thinker, of course, but the breadth and depth of his background played a major role as well. A finance and human resources professional by training, he is also a martial arts instructor, author, photographer, knife maker, and journalist, a rather wide-ranging mix.

Did you notice that IT is not on the list? While he acquired those skills on the job, there are many leaders and subject matter experts in the organization who are far more technical than he will likely ever be. Nevertheless, he is successful because of cross-pollination. Not only does he have an eclectic background, he also a strong professional network and is able to draw upon the talents of diverse individuals from both inside and outside the company (e.g., employees, consultants, educators, suppliers) to perform the work. He has found that knowing what and who to ask is far more important than being able to generate all the answers himself.

Speaking of networking, have you heard the term crowdsourcing? Crowdsourcing is a method of obtaining information by leveraging the creative energy of large numbers of people, typically through the internet. The more creative minds the better, including stakeholders, subject matter experts, and interested parties who have no skin in the game. Done right, crowdsourcing lets you reach out to hundreds of thousands, if not millions of people quickly and reliably. Amazon product reviews are an example, as are the branding tricks that tech-savvy companies like Apple successfully employ. Social media sites such as LinkedIn and Facebook can be used in much the same way, as can business collaboration tools like wikis, SharePoint sites, and the like.

Crowdsourcing primarily leverages input from strangers rather than people you already know, which in some ways makes it even more powerful than solely reaching out to your network. For example, Kane has a professional network of well over a thousand people, not Facebook friends, but actual business contacts. Sounds impressive until you realize that means that there are more than 175,000 people across the United States and in 70 countries in his company alone that he has never met. More than 140,000 of those folks hold college degrees, including roughly 35,000 advanced degrees, in virtually every business and technical field you could think of. There's no way he could ever meet that many folks let alone build relationships with them, yet with crowdsourcing any of those smart people with an interest can weigh in. There is an art to understanding and evaluating inputs to garner useful information, of course, but think of the value all that brainpower can provide when harnessed correctly.

When looking for diverse opinions and perspectives, consider generational differences too. Baby Boomers (born 1946 – 1964), Gen X (born 1965 – 1983), and Millennials (born 1984 – 2002) tend to have different life experiences, desires, and interests, yet they often work together within the same organizations. Growing up shortly after WWII, most Boomers faced more austere childhoods than their Gen X or Millennial counterparts, often translating into different priorities. For instance, in many cases a Boomer's parents baked them a cake and invited a few friends over on their birthdays, whereas their own children might have gone to Chuck E. Cheese's or had a catered party. Consequently, Boomers have a tendency to be more conservative, career-oriented, and focus on things that create and maintain a strong support network. Millennials, on the other hand, tend to be far more technologically savvy, experience-focused, and willing to accept change. These varying viewpoints can be very powerful when brought together.

Sensei, Mentor, Teacher, Coach Tip:

> The power of diversity stems from leveraging the life experiences of people with a variety of different backgrounds and thought processes who come together to solve a common problem. It's not just education or work experience, socio-economic, geographical, racial, ethnic, religious, and generational differences are all examples; whatever generates a variety of perspectives.

Action:

What can you learn from the life of a painter? A musician? A movie producer? How do they see their art? Go get a DVD box set you may have wanted for some time, or if you already own a set you like pull it down and play it with the commentaries on. Streaming video with bonus features will accomplish the same thing. What you're looking for is insight. Listen to the actors and directors talk about their craft, their art. It's a safe bet that they will say something that will jump out, giving you an "ah, ha!" moment. Welcome to cross-pollination.

To take it a step further, if you are not already mentoring someone, seriously consider doing so now. It can take a considerable investment in time and energy to be a good mentor, yet benefits include expanding your network and influence, acquiring insight about your leadership style and effectiveness, gaining greater perspective about the organization's challenges and opportunities, leveraging diverse perspectives, and increasing your effectiveness as well as that of your team. All good stuff, huh? Not only should you be mentoring someone, perhaps several individuals depending on your position and experience, but you should also be a mentee as well.

Particularly in large companies, sponsorship from those above and below makes a tremendous impact on career growth and opportunity. In part this comes from the folks in charge knowing who you are and understanding your capabilities. Irrespective of climbing the career ladder, however, successful leaders always strive to learn from those who have come before. Protégés not only benefit from their mentors' expertise generally, but they also acquire insights into the organization's philosophy, culture, and politics, gain access to resources and support, and become more confident and capable in performing their work.

Mentoring is symbiotic. The process often starts with an informational interview that can help you mutually decide whether or not a mentor/mentee relationship would be beneficial. Ask about the other person's experience, expectations, leadership style, current challenges, and the like. Look for someone you can learn from whose strengths and weaknesses are complimentary to your own, and who you can trust to maintain confidentiality of the relationship. If there appears to be a good fit, subsequent conversations can delve into specific goals and timelines for the relationship. Depending on your objectives, what you are trying to accomplish, mentoring can be a short- or long-term proposition. It is useful to put things in writing, a sort of contract for how you will work and grow together.

Clearly you will need to assure that you have the bandwidth to take on more work (as well as approval from your supervisor where appropriate), but anyone who has an unmet business need you can volunteer to fulfil can make an ideal candidate. You get to do something meaningful while gaining hands-on experience under their tutelage. Recognizing the benefits of this approach, many companies go so far as to build formal mentoring programs and assign mentors at all levels of their leadership team.

Your mentor or protégé need not even be within your organization, however. There are many worthwhile groups or causes you can join to gain experience. You can mentor military leaders transitioning to civilian employment, counsel college graduates entering the workplace, or tutor at-risk youth. If you work for a large bureaucratic organization, consider a smaller, more nimble group you could work with and learn from. Conversely, if you work for a startup that could use an infusion of process discipline, consider a larger, well established group to work with. Non-profit agencies, which come in all shapes and sizes, can be great places to fulfill this need. Since they are perennially understaffed, they tend to welcome help.

For example, Kane was elected to serve on the leadership council at his son's middle school as treasurer and subsequently president of the parent's club. In that capacity he helped a non-profit organization achieve consensus on a variety of challenging issues, including hiring a new principal, resolving personality conflicts amongst school officials, achieving accreditation, and assuring financial accountability. He was able to bring a corporate perspective, rigor, and process discipline to the non-profit while simultaneously gaining experiences and honing skills that helped him become much more successful at his day job. The greater your network, the more diverse your experience, the more you can leverage cross-pollination.

Sensei, Mentor, Teacher, Coach – Little Life Secret:

> By sourcing a position or a statement from a famous person you gain some of their clout. Don't hide your source; share it for everybody's benefit.

14

IMAGE

Four Elements of How You Are Perceived

"People are like stained-glass windows. They sparkle and shine when the sun is out, but when the darkness sets in their true beauty is revealed only if there is a light from within."
Elisabeth Kubler-Ross[30]

Both authors are fans of the Oakland Raiders football team. Often when people hear this they try to build a logical bridge to connect the dots. Most think we must have grown up in Oakland, because being a member or Raider Nation isn't entirely logical, not when you live in Seattle with its own NFL team anyway.

There was no hometown NFL team when we were kids. The closest teams were the San Francisco Forty Niners, who were terrible at the time, the Minnesota Vikings, and the Oakland Raiders. We independently chose the Raiders, followed the games, and even had team posters on our bedroom walls.

When we watched the Raiders defeat the Vikings in Super Bowl XI, well, the deal was made in our hearts. We can still name and talk about the greats, Hendricks, Stabler, Biletnikoff, Allen, Alzado, Plunkett, Long, and many, many more. This love of the Raiders has not diminished by their lack of performance in recent years, nor has it been overridden by the Seahawks' success.

The last few years of Raiders history have been disappointing, but we keep following them because they are "our team." Love is not rational, be it of an organization, a product, or a person. Think about brand loyalty, the old Mac vs. PC argument, Coke vs. Pepsi. If you have deep abiding love for your company, your team, your martial arts system, your instructor, your compatriots, your high school or college, or virtually anything else, the fact of the matter is that relationship is a love affair… and it's not rational. Nevertheless it is also very real.

This brand loyalty tends to begin with convenience and the time in life of the exposure. The closer an item it is to you the more accessible it is, and the more accessible it is the more likely you are to get early and repeated exposure. It is close, it's easy, it's priced right, whatever… we make a choice and then, unless it blows up spectacularly in our faces straight away, we tend to rationalize that choice. Remember the aforementioned first impression bias? What started as convenient becomes ensconced in our minds. Over time it turns into a full blown love affair.

When it comes to martial arts, for example, often the teacher of convenience becomes "one of the best." And then the system becomes "brilliant and all encompassing." Clearly the student has made an excellent choice. So, if you are a martial arts instructor, small business owner, coach, or team leader, the question becomes how do you make sure that your school or organization is that prospective client's excellent choice? How do you get them started on that path toward a love affair?

Think about what you are offering. For instance many Raiders fans are drawn toward the team by their image: iconic silver and black, eye patch, and crossed swords. It's cool. It seems shallow, perhaps, but image matters. For example, Kane often wears a silver skull bracelet. It is a heavy, outlaw biker-looking piece that accessorizes nicely with a Raider's jersey, but in reality he sees it as a symbol of impermanence, a reminder to prioritize, focus on the right things, and create a worthy legacy to leave behind when he's gone. While it makes an odd contrast with a business suit, it can also be a conversation starter with other sourcing professionals when he makes quips like, "These are all the prospective suppliers who wouldn't agree to our Terms & Conditions." Nevertheless, there are certain situations where he leaves the jewelry behind because it would set the wrong impression.

Let's break it down a bit, covering the four key elements to how you are perceived by others: (1) Appearance, (2) Demeanor, (3) Attire, and (4) Behavior. Each of these elements projects an image, but not always what you think. We're not here to argue right or wrong in this instance. Your image is up to you. But, the image you choose should be an intentional one.

1. Appearance:

Appearance is what you look like. Consider how many business executives are tall, handsome, and impeccably groomed. It's not fair, but it's a fact that certain people have an inherent genetic advantage over others. Nevertheless, you can do a lot about your appearance even if you were not blessed with movie-star good looks. Clearly you can and should make conscious choices about things like hairstyle, visible tattoos, piercings, facial hair, and the like. That's what folks tend to spot first, even subtle stuff like whether or not you have chapped lips and how neatly you trim and/or paint your fingernails.

That's an easy place to start, but let's consider the whole package too. Taller people are automatically given more respect than shorter people, yet a short person with good posture is often perceived as taller than a big person with bad posture. Athletic people are taken more seriously than the obese ones, so maintain a healthy lifestyle and get plenty of exercise. There is medical proof (from Professor Richard Restak at the George Washington University School of Medicine and Heath Sciences) that obesity and lack of physical activity are detrimental to the brain's cognitive abilities, so staying in shape keeps you mentally sound too. Perceptions of physical appearance, skin, hair, proportionality, and the like stem from cues about your general health, all of which can impact what folks think about you. And, most of which you can control.

2. Demeanor:

Demeanor is what you try to look like, your expression. Most communication is non-verbal, so expression is our primary means of conveying intent to others. Not words, demeanor. In an obvious example, if someone who is crying says, "Everything is fine," we do not trust the words. The rate, tone, pitch, and volume of your voice helps people understand your emotion, which in turn gives cues to your intent. But, it is overridden by body language when not congruent. Since most folks are instinctively good at reading expressions, demeanor plays a powerful role in communication.

Actors are adept at faking body language, but most of us are not trained performers so people see right through us when we try. Not only are we far more transparent than we think, we oftentimes convey a different message than intended. For example, restlessness can be read as eagerness or as nervous fear, depending on the degree. Relaxed body language can seem a sign of cool competence, or of ignorance or laziness. Even how you breathe plays a role. Low, slow abdominal breaths exude competence and confidence such as you might find with elite operators or martial artists, whereas breathing high and fast in the chest indicates fear or bluster.

It can be very valuable to join an organization like Toastmasters where you can hone your communication skills, particularly if you need to do a lot of public speaking. Even if the biggest group you talk to consists of one or two other individuals, however, being a good communicator is beneficial. Simple things like leaning forward with an open expression when listening can make a world of difference in how you are perceived.

3. **Attire:**

How you dress says a lot about you. It can tell people about your ethnic origin (e.g., *hijab*, *keffiyeh*, tartan), give hints to your religion (e.g., *yarmulke*, crucifix, Thor's hammer), your socioeconomic status (e.g., Wrangler, Levis, Jordache), your membership in a group (e.g., red or blue scarves, Masonic rings), or your profession (e.g., uniform, surgical scrubs). It can even indicate something about your values such as what is more important to you, comfort or appearance, or whether it is more valuable to blend in or stand out.

Regardless of your physical beauty, intelligence, or physique, neatly pressed clothing conveys a different impression than a rumpled appearance. College and professional basketball and football players are often required to wear suits and ties on their way to and from games in order to present a dignified impression. Wearing your underwear on the outside, "sagging," and the like conveys the exact opposite.

Be aware of the messages that your attire conveys. For example, a martial arts instructor whose uniform is covered in patches and "bling" gives a very different impression than one whose starched white *gi* is devoid of ostentation. Ever seen the movie *Napoleon Dynamite*? We all laughed at Rex Kwon Do with his red, white, and blue uniform all covered in stars and stripes, even those who have never taken a martial arts class. You probably don't want to be a caricature.

Wilder wants to blend in when he travels, "I don't wear a baseball cap, it says 'American,' nor do I wear tennis shoes, another dead giveaway. My shirts don't have a logo. I prefer to be as non-nondescript as possible in most instances. My goal is to move through space with the least amount of friction. Of course when I hit the seminar floor and I'm teaching— well, I'm in a pressed white *gi* with my *obi* wrapped around my waist."

Many professionals are required to wear uniforms that represent their organization, outfits that convey an image the group wants to portray. You can see this in everything from various branches of military service or law enforcement to McDonald's crewmembers and UPS delivery drivers. Sports teams do the same thing with their jerseys. These distinctive styles are designed with forethought to communicate at a glance who the folks that wear them are and what they represent.

For example, when working stadium security, Kane took advantage of a uniform, radio, clipboard, and credentials to convey authority. He did not have to explain who he was when resolving problems; it was pretty obvious even to the drunk and disorderly. Using appearance and voice alone he was able to break up a lot of fights, whereas in another setting without that official attire he would have to go hands on to get them same result.

Pay attention not only to the attire, but also to how it is worn. For example, professional football players are required to wear identical outfits that match from helmet to socks, even shoe colors and helmet markings are proscribed, and to tuck in their jerseys during game play. They can be fined for any deviation from the NFL's strict uniform code. College players, on the other hand, have fewer restrictions. In some cases coaches let team members wear their jerseys untucked, creating slovenly appearance. We are not aware of any scientific study on the subject, but anecdotal evidence suggests that disorderly appearance is often reflected in sloppy game play, excessive penalties, and other mistakes, perhaps due in part to referees reacting to the image that is portrayed on the field.

4. Behavior:

Behavior, appearance, and speech interact. Lots of things come out naturally in your behavior. For example, how you move gives insight to your physicality, your comfort with yourself, and how you feel about other people. How you stand shows whether you are prepared or unprepared, if you are on top of things or lax.

Non-verbal behavior sends a powerful message when communicating with others. Some folks, especially those who are kinesthetic learners, tend to have body language that is naturally dismissive of others even when they are paying rapt attention. Are you multi-tasking or actively listening, making direct eye contact or staring off into space, leaning forward or sitting back with your arms crossed? To be perceived as sincere, it is vital to be aware of how you are coming across and have as congruent of a message as possible.

Don't forget about social media. Posting video from your bachelor party might be titillating for your friends, but what about prospective employers, employees, landlords, or students? In today's connected world it is easier to find out about you than ever before. We're not suggesting that you change your core personality, but rather that you be thoughtful about your image. Carefully consider what you do in public places where others may record your actions as well. Even if you don't post something salacious online, chances are good that if it was done in public somebody else just might.

Image is an admixture of appearance, demeanor, attire, and behavior, all factors that you control to large degree. What you do, the manner in which you dress, how you act and react—purposeful or not these elements all play powerful roles in how others perceive you. Perception being reality in most instances, this means that image can help or hinder your ability to meet personal and professional goals. Choose wisely.

Sensei, Mentor, Teacher, Coach Tip:

> Leaders who are viewed as cold, calculating, or indifferent have a very hard time getting anything done even when they are earnest and forthright. Since nonverbal communication trumps words, it is imperative to be conscious and considered about the impression you give.

Action:

There are many great books on body language, such as *The Silent Language of Leaders: How Body Language Can Help—or Hurt—How You Lead* by Carol Kinsey Goman, *What Every BODY is Saying: An Ex-FBI Agent's Guide to Speed-Reading People* by Joe Navarro and Marvin Karlins, or even *Body Language for Dummies* by Elizabeth Kuhnke. There are also many, many websites that you can source for free too. Take a look at these resources and identify what you are doing that is beneficial or harmful to your cause when interacting with others.

For example, think about your hand and arm movements. Crossing your arms while sitting makes you appear guarded, self-conscious, or closed off, even if it's just habitual, whereas doing the same thing while standing can make you appear callous, coldhearted, or confrontational. In a traditional martial arts setting, crossing your arms is not only disrespectful it is often interpreted as a challenge, so doing it in an old school *dojo* could actually lead to a fight. Clenched fists, often construed as a sign of anger, fear, or nervousness, can add to the impression.

What do you do with your eyes? Many people will judge you by how you make eye contact (or don't) alone. Depending on your culture, direct eye contact may not be the norm. Nevertheless, looking down a lot will make you appear timid or shy. Sideways glances make you appear nervous, distracted, or deceitful, whereas looking askance indicates distrust. Furtive or lingering glances at certain portions of another person's anatomy can send a strong message too.

If you are ready for deeper insight, perhaps the most severe version of this drill, pull the body language information from one of the sources listed above, hand it to the closest person you know and trust, and ask, "What do I do on this list?" Then stand back and listen… You may be surprised by the results.

Sensei, Mentor, Teacher, Coach – Little Life Secret:

> Colors can affect how you are perceived. There are two basic skin tones, warm and cool. A neat trick for identifying which category you fit into is to look at the veins underneath your arm. If they show blue through your skin you have cool tones, whereas if they are more greenish in appearance you have warm tones. Knowing your skin tones can help you select clothing (and cosmetics) that augment your appearance. Be aware of what you wear where, however. For example, the wrong color clothing can incite hostility or violence at a sporting event even if you aren't rooting for the other team.

15

THE RIGHT WORDS

Verbiage is More Important than You Might Think

"Nobody cares how much you know, until they know how much you care."
Theodore Roosevelt[31]

When he arrived at school to pick up his son one afternoon, Wilder noticed two other cars of the same make and model parked next to him. On the drive home Wilder's son checked his Facebook account remarking, "Hey dad, look at this picture of the school parking lot that Susan posted, it is three cars just like yours." Wilder responded that he noticed the three car anomaly too, and asked what Susan had written. "She says three primary color cars." When they got to a stoplight Wilder looked at the picture, surprised to notice that there was a red, a yellow, and a blue car, all primary colors, and all the same make and model. Wilder had noticed three cars whereas Susan had perceived the colors they were painted.

Men and women see the world differently. They have different brain chemistry, hence have a tendency to process information and respond to words in different ways. What motivates a man is not as likely to motivate a woman and vice versa. This is neither a bad thing nor a good thing, just a difference—different brains, different needs.

There are numerous examples of gender brain differences, but we won't bury you with multiple proof points. Nevertheless, we do want to touch on a study done by Larry Cahill, a professor of Neurobiology and Behavior at the School of Biological Sciences at the University of California, Irvine. His research, *Sex-Related Difference in Amygdala Activity during Emotionally Influenced Memory Storage* published in November, 2000, showed that brains of men and women respond differently to horror films by tracking neural activity in the amygdala. Located deep in the temporal lobes of the brain (behind the eyes and about where your temples are), the amygdala controls emotional reactions.

Professor Cahill was able to demonstrate that when the male subjects were exposed to a horror film, the left side of their amygdala lit-up. That side is responsible for accounting for the basics of the event a person is witnessing, the essence of the moment. When women were exposed to the same scene, however, the opposite side of their amygdala fired. The right side of the amygdala is in charge of the details of the moment.

The results might be that when a couple sits in a theater watching a scary movie, the boyfriend is thinking about what the characters should be doing to get out of the house, clear the threat, and escape to safety. The girlfriend, on the other hand, is noticing that the distribution of the blood splatter that was on the left side of the actor's face in the previous scene has suddenly switched sides due to an editing error… all while simultaneously trying to figure out how to clear the threat and escape to safety. Different responses by gender to the same stress, the same information, make it evident that although the same general area of the brain is engaged, the location utilized varies so the reactions are different.

Communication is a haphazard endeavor at the best of times. What's said and heard are rarely the same thing as few individuals are fully engaged in any given conversation, yet in times of stress it degrades even farther. For example, when a group of nurses or orderlies in a mental hospital has to physically restrain a patient who has gotten out of control, they often use physical cues as well as words to communicate with each other. Not only do they get commands like, "Move over, I can help," but also they often get a tap or push as well.

The reason for this multi-layered communication is an attempt to circumvent the adverse impact of adrenaline. Stress can cause a loss of fine motor skills such as finger dexterity, complex motor skills such as hand-eye coordination, and depth perception. Under extreme conditions, people experience hyper-vigilance, loss of rational thought, memory loss, and inability to consciously move or react, but fortunately most of us do not have to deal with such situations.

It is important to note, however, that male and female adrenal dumps work differently. Men experience a rapid spike and quick fall off, whereas adrenaline takes much longer to kick in for women and falls off much more slowly. This means that, among other things, women can be more level-headed at the beginning of a crisis, but also that men can reach the positive aspects such as increased strength and pain resistance much quicker.

Studies performed by Simon Baron-Cohen, Director of the Autism Research Center at Cambridge University, show that that distinctions between male and female brains stem from biology rather than culture. While men have about four percent more brain cells on average, women tend to have more dendritic connections between cells, a larger corpus collosum (which allows for faster data transfer between hemispheres), and a larger limbic system (which allows for better understanding and expression of feelings). Consequently, men tend to be better at analyzing systems whereas women tend to be more in tune with their feelings and better at reading the emotions of other people.

Similarly, there is a difference in gender when it comes to teaching. Men and women respond differently to coaching and mentoring. There are many ways to approach this but one of the simpler and most direct ways to be successful is to understand the way the genders generally desire things:

- Most men want to know that they are strong and also that they are at the very least competent. Men can live with not being the best at everything, but if you look closely you will see that men will carve out a niche in which they are proficient. So, if work doesn't reflect this competency, a hobby will.

- Most women, on the other hand, prefer to be beautiful and loved. They don't have to be the most beautiful woman in the room, but they do need to be the most beautiful to those that they love and who love them back. In our experience there is no greater love or joy exchanged than that of a young child with and for his or her mother. The mother is the most beautiful person in the world to the child and vice versa. This illustrates the point we are making.

Because the mind hears the action and the noun, Wilder uses a communication trick when talking with students of different genders to assure that they understand his intent. Let's say that he wants to compliment the student for performing a properly executed karate punch, here is an example of how the two different approaches might work:

Men: *"Jason, that was a strong punch, solid form."*

Women: *"Laura, that was a beautiful punch, good form."*

Jason heard the words, "strong" and "solid" whereas Laura heard, "beautiful" and "good." This is an example of speaking to the genders in different words in order to obtain the same result, clear communication.

Finding the right words can be tough enough at the best of times, yet in stressful situations it can be a significant challenge. A great resource is the book *Effective Phrases for Performance Appraisals: A Guide to Successful Evaluations* by James E. Neal, Jr. While written for a specific managerial responsibility, the concepts apply broadly. Additionally, here is a short list of words that you can use to spark the right conversation:

The Right Words

- Strength
- Confidence
- Goals
- Consistency
- Imagination
- Believe
- Challenge
- Fulfillment
- Risk
- Pride
- Discipline
- Drive

- Hard work
- Action
- Joy
- Passion
- Knowledge
- Overcome
- Role model
- Encouragement
- Own it
- Great
- Control
- Action

Choosing the right words is important, but you must also consider your audience when you speak in order to select the right approach. For example, many business executives prefer a "be bright, be brief, be gone" methodology, whereas many lower level managers and technical employees feel a need to know and analyze all the relevant details. This phenomenon is associated to brain type differences, which we'll cover in the next chapter, but is also tied to demands of the job. The discrepancy, which can be boiled down to inductive versus deductive communication style preferences, is often a source of conflict. It doesn't need to be.

If your boss is not a detail guy or gal, but you are, remember that you were hired for a reason. The boss is counting on you to have performed the appropriate analysis, but does not necessarily need or want to know everything, just enough to understand and approve or disapprove your recommendations. Or to communicate them further up the food chain. Start with the answer, whatever you are proposing, and if the boss agrees you're done. Once you get a yes, stop selling your solution. If more information is needed, on the other hand, you can walk him or her through the processes of how you got there.

Regardless of the level of detail expected, knowing where you are leading to will help clarify your arguments and tighten up the conversation. It works much like a common practice in behavioral interviewing where applicants are asked to answer questions in the form of a STAR, an acronym that stands for (1) Situation, (2) Task, (3) Action, and (4) Result. Using the STAR technique forces a logical, structured response that can crisply explain what occurred, giving interviewers pertinent information necessary to evaluate and differentiate candidates. If this sort of thing does not come naturally, it is valuable to rehearse what you plan to say before speaking with executives much like you would before addressing a large group. The more organized and prepared you are, the better you will come across and the more effective your communication will be.

One of the challenges that many of us face is accepting "no" for an answer at work. We are passionate and knowledgeable about whatever we do for a living, yet the boss does not always see things our way. Sometimes that is because he or she knows something that we don't, perhaps something confidential that cannot be shared. Other times it's merely a difference of opinion. Either way, the boss is still the boss; ultimately it's his or her prerogative to decide and our responsibility to support. Few things are as career-limiting as expressing sour grapes behind the boss's back.

Regardless, disagreements shouldn't sour relationships unless the other person is being completely unreasonable and perhaps not even then. A good rule of thumb is that if the boss understands your concerns, restating your argument in his or her own words, but still disagrees with your opinion it's time to stop pushing. On the other hand, if it's clear that he or she is missing a pertinent piece of information, more explanation is appropriate. Their job is to listen, understand, and decide, whereas yours is to provide pertinent facts and data for prudent decision-making.

Regardless of whether you're the ultimate decision-maker or the subordinate, clarifying expectations makes a tremendous difference in how well you communicate. Agreeing to methods and roles of working together early in a relationship can significantly reduce conflict.

On or off the job, words can spark conflict in all aspects of your life. Being sanctimonious, condescending, dogmatic, or derogatory tends to get other people's dander up rather quickly. Nevertheless, as easily as the wrong words can start a quarrel, the right ones can end it. For example, if you are in error about something, admit it. We all know that honesty is a much better way to de-escalate a bad situation than lying or stubbornly refusing to acknowledge a wrong, yet oftentimes we let our ego get in the way. In a professional work environment that kind of behavior can spark resentment and covert retaliation, whereas in other situations it can lead to physical violence.

Try not to insult or embarrass other people, particularly in public. We do not like being treated that way, we are pretty sure you do not either, and strongly suspect that neither will an aggressive person who already has a beef with you because of something you've said or done. Giving someone a face-saving way out affords them the opportunity to back down gracefully without feeling the need to lash out in order salvage lost dignity or honor. Praise publically, criticize privately.

Sensei, Mentor, Teacher, Coach Tip:

> Generally people don't hear the modifiers in conversations. Similar to predictive typing used by many computer applications and smartphones, the human mind makes general assumptions about the sentence that has just been said, oftentimes glossing over the modifiers and focusing only on the subjects and actions in the sentence.

Action:

Whenever possible speak in positive terms. The classic example is the coach who says, "Don't fumble the football," instead of using the more constructive approach, "Hang on to the ball." The challenge with the former approach is that the player's subconscious more often than not hears "fumble the ball" rather than the intended opposite. When correcting a student or employee it is often easy to say, "Don't do...," and that approach has its place, however positive terms are more effective in most instances. "Do more of this and less of that" is a good general template with which to start. It's harder to misunderstand a critique, and far easier to accept feedback, when it comes across as constructive.

Beyond positive and negative speech patterns, think about implications of what you say when interacting with others. Oftentimes habitual turns of phrase come back to haunt you. For example, saying something along the lines of, "Let me be honest with you," or "Truthfully…," implies that up until that point in the conversation you have been deceitful, even when you were completely forthright. Similarly, saying "I'll try" can come across as dissembling. You either will or you won't. If you cannot commit to something, don't tap dance. Provide an alternative proposal, say no, negotiate the due date, or whatever is most appropriate, but don't "lawyer-up" unless there's an incredibly good reason for doing so. It makes you appear untrustworthy.

Furthermore, minimize statements that convey uncertainty when speaking. Ambiguous words like "kinda," "sorta," and the like have their place, particularly amongst friends, but they come across as indecisive in professional settings, hence can undermine your credibility. Everyone stumbles from time to time, especially when searching for the exact right words to convey a thought, but excessive use of "um," "uh," and "and" will make you seem insecure.

Words matter, learn to channel them to further your aspirations. Work with a coach or mentor, record yourself speaking (where legally able to), ask for feedback from your team, or consider membership in a group like Toastmasters to hone your skills. Leaders who communicate in a cogent and pithy manner are far more effective at supporting, harnessing, and growing the talents of those around them.

Sensei, Mentor, Teacher, Coach – Little Life Secret:

> The word "problem" implies great difficulties, something seemingly insurmountable. The word "challenge," on the other hand, implies something more easily overcome. Replace the word problem with the word challenge in your vocabulary and you will be seen as a more optimistic individual. It helps place you in the mindset to identify creative solutions too.

16

BRAIN TYPING

Chess Trumps Checkers When It Comes to Personnel

"There is no substitute for accurate knowledge. Know yourself, know your business, know your men."
Lee Iacocca[32]

We all know that checkers and chess both use exactly the same game board, yet the rules are significantly different. In checkers, all pieces are treated the same, hence become interchangeable. This drives very different strategies than we find in chess where we are able to make use of the unique strengths and weaknesses of the various pieces to play the game. While high performing organizations use their human resources like chess pieces, all too many groups play checkers with their personnel, forgoing the unique leverage afforded by optimally utilizing the knowledge, skills, and experience of each individual. This does a disservice to both the people and the organization.

As an athlete, Mike Reid was a big, scary guy. In 1967, while in college at Penn State, he won the Eastern heavyweight wrestling title. Two years later he led the Nittany Lions' defense with 89 tackles, was voted a unanimous All-America and All-East defensive end, finished fifth overall in Heisman Trophy balloting, and was subsequently elected to the College Football Hall of Fame. Drafted in the first round (#7 overall) by the Cincinnati Bengals, he played four years in the NFL where he was twice selected to the Pro Bowl.

An extraordinary athlete with an adroit mind, when he left the Cincinnati Bengals he held the team record for sacks. As imposing as Reid was on the football field, you might be surprised to know that he studied music in college and eventually became a Grammy Award-winning country music star. His song, "Walk of Faith" was a Billboard number one hit.

While people may have seen Mike Reid as a rough-and-tumble football player, his music career showed another, softer side. The old saying goes, "You can't judge a book by its cover." True enough; to really get to know a person, to leverage the best they have to offer, you need to know and understand their brain.

As aspiring athletes begin their journey into sports the discrepancy amongst individuals is profound. Some kids hit puberty earlier than others, resulting in an inherent muscle mass advantage. These kids become stronger and larger, while the late-bloomers' biological clocks tick away at a slower rate. Yet unless they join a league that segregates athletes by age *and* weight, they all compete in the same sports teams and physical education classes.

Even prior to puberty, genetics play a role in athletic development. Being inherently taller or a larger-boned due to one's parents can create a natural advantage since the biggest kid on the field, in the martial arts studio, or even in the classroom is often seen differently than the smallest. They can frequently do more and perform better. Nevertheless, education tends to level the playing field as we move from youthful athletic competition into the adult world. Education is about the brain.

The brain and its natural predispositions is a determining factor in every aspect of human endeavor. As children move up and through levels of athletic competition they tend to become more specialized, just as when we move into the work force we also become more specialized, skilled, and hopefully more adroit in our chosen field. While natural physicality is always a factor for athletes, the brain becomes the determining factor of who can achieve the highest levels of success and who cannot.

Sound incongruous? Let's tease this out a bit…

At the first rung of baseball for kids we find T-Ball. Players bat the ball off of a chest-high tee, like a giant golfer, because most children at this age have no ability to hit a ball pitched at them let alone be the one accurately throwing it over the plate. As they move up the ladder of competition and enter Pee Wee leagues, they begin to specialize. This is where a kid might find himself batting in the fourth position, called "clean up," because he has the potential to hit a home run clearing the three loaded bases of batters who went before him. This position is often earned simply because that particular player happens to be the biggest, strongest kid on the team. This is also where a larger child might become the catcher because he or she can effectually block home plate from the runner coming from third, stopping a score.

As they move into high school and the competition becomes more advanced, that same big kid might find himself playing first base because, in our example, he happens to be left-handed. Physical disparity amongst players begins to disappear as young people gain in age, muscle mass, and understanding, and the attitude of the athlete begins to rise as a factor of their performance as well.

On a high-performing college baseball team there may be two or three Major League caliber players. When these folks move into the minor leagues and eventually (with skill and a little luck) into the Majors, they will be surrounded by professionals, every last one of them. Now both attitude and brain type become the margins between success and failure. We argue that it is the same in the business world too, only the score is kept in dollars and cents, patents and inventions, not displayed on a Jumbotron for the crowd to see.

Understanding the brain types of who you are working with and responsible for is a great tool that should not be overlooked. With brain typing you can help the little league player, the college athlete, or the young woman in shipping at your office. And you can use it to help yourself too. The science behind this was popularized by Jon Niednagel, President of the Brain Typing Institute. Volunteering as a youth soccer coach, he noticed that players who behaved similarly also had similar athletic techniques. From there, he began to connect the Myers-Briggs Type Indicator® (MBTI) brain types to athletic performance.

The MBTI was developed by the mother and daughter combination of Isabel Myers and Katherine Briggs in an effort to operationalize the theories of renowned psychiatrist Karl Jung. It was used during World War II for successfully placing civilians in jobs required by the war effort and has been refined several times since. Constantly being tested for validity and reliability, it has been widely adopted by businesses and academic institutions today. The theory goes that each person is born with one of 16 brain types. These types, also called brain wirings or designs, are based on four basic pairs of psychological attributes:

- Extroverted (E) vs. Introverted (I)
- Sensing (S) vs. iNtuitive (N)
- Thinking (T) vs. Feeling (F)
- Judging (J) vs. Perceiving (P)

You'll note that the second letter of the word intuitive is capitalized to avoid confusion with the word introverted, since both start with the same letter. That is intentional, not a typo. Everyone falls somewhere along each of these four continua, a predilection that can easily be evaluated via a personality test. Each brain type combination has inherent strengths and specific weaknesses, qualities that affect all aspects of a person's life and are particularly apparent in physical endeavors.

With over twenty years of research on psychology, neuroscience, and biology, Niednagel codified his theories and became an adviser for professional sports teams throughout the United States. In one of his most famous predictions, he helped the Indianapolis Colts select Peyton Manning (ESTP) in the 1998 NFL draft, stating that he would become a top performing quarterback in the NFL, whereas Ryan Leaf (ESTJ) would be much less successful because of his personality type.

Anyone who follows American football knows how incredibly well that selection worked out. For those who don't, Manning still plays pro ball fifteen years later, currently for the Denver Broncos. Former number two overall draft pick Leaf, on the other hand, had a short-lived professional career that earned him the reputation as one of the biggest busts in NFL history. Since leaving football he has had several run-ins with the law, including a 2012 arrest for breaking into two houses and stealing painkillers while on probation. In 2013 he was moved from a drug treatment center to the Montana State Prison for threatening a staff member and other behavioral problems according to news reports.

When you discover that athletes' personalities can be assessed through their body motions on the field, you begin to realize that psychological type has its underpinnings not only in the brain, but throughout one's entire body. This is powerful information. Niednagel has been able to identify athletes' personality types in mere minutes simply by watching how they move. He also uses electroencephalography (EEG) scans for verification from time to time, relying on hard science to augment psychological theory. Under the EEG it is possible to see that different personality types use certain regions of their brains differently.

For predicting athletic performance Niednagel organizes MBTI personality types by their middle two letters since those are the ones that most affect physical skills. In other words:

- SFs (Sensing-Feeling) tend to be gross-motor skilled
- STs (Sensing-Thinking) tend to be fine-motor skilled
- NFs (iNtuitive-Feeling) tend to be speech-skilled
- NTs (iNtuitive-Thinking) tend to be voice-skilled and adept at logical abstraction

Professional athletes and coaches alike have gravitated toward this approach because it works quite well. For example, the best clutch players in the NBA tend to be ISTPs, folks like Larry Bird, Michael Jordan, Pete Maravich, Hakeem Olajuwon, John Stockton, Bill Walton, and Jerry West. Knowing that ahead of time helps coaches place players in the optimal position to take advantage of both their physicality and brain type.

While brain type plays a vital role in helping an athlete meet his or her full potential, it is by no means the only thing that matters. Research shows that roughly 60% of athletic ability stems from personality predilections, whereas the remaining 40% comes from environmental factors such as team cohesion and effective coaching which you can control, and the way the person was raised, their value system, and support from family and friends over which you will have minimal, if any, influence.

Another advantage of understanding the brain types of those around you is in facilitating communication. While it is impossible to accommodate all styles simultaneously, it is valuable to understand and consider personality predilections whenever practicable. This applies for teaching, mentoring, and coaching:

- **Extraversion** (E): successful strategies for working with extraverts generally include interactive assignments using collaborative work groups, freeform discussions or debates to exchange information and stimulate learning. These folks often prefer oral communication over written.
- **Introversion** (I): for introverts it is important to integrate and connect subject matter, using logical chunks of interconnected facts. These individuals generally prefer to think and reflect on work, excelling at written assignments while being challenged by interactive discussions. When debate is required, allow sufficient think time for Introverts to deliberate ahead of time.
- **iNtuition** (N): intuitive people like more generalized concept maps and learn well using a "theory–application–theory" approach. These individuals are comfortable working with hunches and other unexplainable ways of knowing, looking for patterns, meanings, and future possibilities. While they excel at creative assignments, they are often bored by, and resistant to, routines.
- **Sensing** (S): strategies for interacting with sensing individuals include organized, linear, structured discussions conducted in an "application–theory–application" approach. These folks tend to appreciate early understanding of objectives so that they can prepare for what they must know or do in advance. They prefer to work with givens in the real world rather than with abstract theories or possibilities.

- **Thinking** (T): thinking individuals generally focus on facts and data. They strongly believe in, and generally want to comply with, objectives, principles, and policies and may have trouble working "outside of the box." They have a strong preference for organizing and structuring information in logical, clear, and objective ways, and working toward precise, action-oriented assignments.
- **Feeling** (F): feeling individuals tend to be subjective, values-based people, who focus on emotion rather than fact. They have preferences for organizing and structuring information in a personal, value-oriented ways. Successful strategies for working with these individuals include interactive group activities, open discussions, and harmonious social interactions.
- **Perceiving** (P): because individuals who prefer perceiving are flexible and open to experience, they often have many things going on at once but do not always follow through. Successful strategies for these folks include breaking assignments into small steps with interim deadlines to assure completion. These individuals excel in situations that allow for spontaneity and creativity.
- **Judging** (J): people who prefer judging like to analyze, organize, and respond, often testing conventional theory. They are goal oriented and enjoy situations that are organized and scheduled. Leaders who play the "devil's advocate" and encourage reverse questioning or debate are often appreciated. Assignments for such individuals should be well-structured with activities and timeframes prearranged.

When you are not dealing with folks one-on-one or in small groups of like-minded individuals, it is particularly helpful to focus on only two of the scales, Extraversion (E) vs. Introversion (I), and Sensing (S) vs. iNtuition (N). These scales have wide ranges, so while folks gravitate one way or the other they are not all exactly alike. Nevertheless, these predilections are almost always visible if you know how to look for them. Here's how it works:

- **Extraverted** (E) people draw energy from outside themselves, thriving on interactions with people, activities, and things. They actively participate, ask questions, and get involved. They also have a tendency to monopolize your time and attention by asking a disproportional number of questions or engaging in prolonged discussions.
- **Introverted** (I) people, on the other hand, draw energy from their internal world of ideas, emotions, and impressions. They tend to be reflection oriented, learning best in a "think–do–think" environment. Even when they are thoroughly engaged, they may appear distant, distracted, or a step behind the others. Introverts are often uncomfortable asking for help and must sometimes be actively drawn into conversations.
- **Sensing** (S) individuals naturally gravitate toward the practical and the immediate. Their learning styles are characterized by a preference for direct, concrete experiences, moderate to high degrees of structure, linear or sequential learning, and a need to know why before doing something. They are often less independent in thought and judgment and may require frequent coaching or direction.
- **iNtuitive** (N) individuals are generally "big picture" types who prefer to focus on imaginative possibilities rather than on concrete realities. This personality type likes to move from theory to practice, typically disliking highly structured environments. They readily accommodate ambiguity, demonstrating a large degree of autonomy and valuing knowledge for its own sake.

In practical reality for group communication, this means striking a balance that maintains enthusiasm and participation from extraverts while actively engaging reticent introverts whose needs might easily be overlooked if they do not speak up. Affording folks the opportunity to read and digest materials ahead of time whenever possible can help draw everyone into the conversation. Overseeing activities and assignments in a manner compatible with the level of autonomy and structure your team feels comfortable with is a good place to begin, but be careful not to over-accommodate in a manner that lets folks become detrimentally locked into their comfort zone. A predilection is a preference, not an absolute. Consciously mixing personality types to leverage their diversity will virtually always facilitate team achievement as well.

By understanding brain types of those in their charge, teachers, coaches, and mentors can communicate better with their teams. Further, they can best align personnel with assignments or positions where they are most likely to excel, one of many ways to leverage a team or organization's strengths and shore up their weaknesses. In this manner you are effectively playing chess instead of checkers with your personnel.

Sensei, Mentor, Teacher, Coach Tip:

> Your brain type changes over time. What you value in life and how you approach it transforms. As adults we may enjoy a good merlot wine, whereas as a teenager we liked Dr. Pepper. Be aware that brain plasticity, age, responsibility, and social environment can change your brain in many ways, some of which may show up on a personality test.

Action:

There are lots of online personality tests, and many are valid, yet as stated previously we prefer the Myers-Briggs model as we have found it consistently reliable, insightful, and actionable. You can take the test on a variety of sites, yet some require registration or charge a fee to take the test. The link we suggest, 16 Personalities (www.16personalities.com), is a great resource. It can be as in-depth as you wish to go, suggesting career paths, work methods, and relationship styles. Importantly, it is personal, private, and free. You can also visit the following web sites for more information on MBTI: www.advisorteam.com, www.keirsey.com, or www.capt.org.

Take the MBTI test, and if you can, have the folks in your organization take the test as well. Share the information and context on how to use it with all involved. Insight is a two way street. When you understand the predilections of those around you it becomes possible to interact more effectively and on a much more meaningful level.

Sensei, Mentor, Teacher, Coach – Little Life Secret:

> Brain types are predilections, not immutable traits. Kane once worked for a vice president who completely misunderstood how to use MBTI information, hence promulgated that all teams be comprised of a specific combination of personality types. It should come as no surprise that the mandate was a spectacular failure, rescinded after three or four months to the embarrassment of the guy who issued the order. It is important to understand this information, but at the same time not to become bound by it.

17

RECOGNIZING EFFORT

Five Fundamentals of the Morale Imperative

"The magic formula that successful businesses have discovered is to treat customers like guests and employees like people."
Tom Peters[33]

While at a summer football camp at a university, Wilder watched the practices his son and some acquaintances ran through. The university was run by a FCS (Football Championship Series) school. They were two years past their National Championship season and had made it to the quarter-finals recently. The coaches and the assisting staff where on their game, crisp, direct and oozing with the sharp focus of a group that had tasted the highest levels of achievement in their field. They wanted more. And they brought that attitude to every practice. Of the hundreds of kids in attendance, only a handful showed glimpses of skills that would possibly land them on a college roster, yet the coaches expected greatness out of each and every player nevertheless.

The linemen were called to begin the Oklahoma Drill, a staple of full-contact football training. Players make a circle inside which two at a time duel for dominance. It is both a physical and mental test, one in which one player wins and another one loses in front of their peers. The drill began with flurry of movement and explosion of sound, whoops and yells, pads clashing, helmets cracking, the more intense the battle, the greater the response from the ring of players watching.

The coaches' whistles and voices served as the tools of control as they oversaw the structured mayhem. Intense frenzy, bruised bodies and egos, punctuated by shouts of encouragement, acknowledgments of success and sometimes of loss, players eagerly scrambled for their turn to prove themselves. Then out of the coach's mouth came a condescending shellacking of popular American society, "Come on, play like a winner. We're all winners now, this is America—everybody gets a trophy."

That comment was not lost on the players. The intensity jumped up a couple of notches as did the level of competition. No one wanted to be a "participation trophy" player. To Wilder's eye, no player failed to answer the call to have pride, to earn it, to give the best they could in front of their coach and their peers.

Recognizing effort does not necessary mean recognizing the best. It does, however, mean acknowledging the best that one has to give, even if that "best" is not good enough. Sometime the greatest effort that a person can give is not what is needed for the moment but that does not mean that they have failed.

A meritocracy is a system, often social, that chooses the talented, the adroit, the people who apply themselves to move forward on the basis of what they have accomplished, their record. Birthright and social status are of little concern to a meritocracy; skill, smarts, and achievements are the factors that matter. The opposite of a meritocracy is egalitarianism. The egalitarian system promulgates that people should receive the same rewards, be treated as equals, and that all people are fundamentally the same in worth as well as in moral status.

Meritocracy can build you a great sports team, as all the best players compete for each position and the elite player earns the starting spot. Pure meritocracy is a harsh environment of black and white, with little room for subtlety. You are either the best or you are not. People are comprised of subtlety, known and understood as well as cloaked and obfuscated. This dynamic is external and internal both, seen and unseen by the observer and the subject alike. Egalitarian behavior, on the other hand says that everybody gets a shot, all people are valuable and the proverbial level playing field is always in play. In most instances this means that effort is valued over results, which of course, creates a regression to the mean.

Recognizing Effort

Neither system is correct. A blend of the two is necessary. Give everyone a shot, value performance, and place the right people in the right roles for success. As a mentor, teacher, or coach you are charged with getting the best out of the folks in your sphere of influence. To perform at a high level much of their motivation needs to be intrinsically based, yet extrinsic forces can make a significant difference. The way you communicate with and recognize your team members plays a vital role.

For example, Kane's son is a high school varsity quarterback. He suffered a significant injury in the pre-season, a medial collateral ligament tear and anterior cruciate ligament sprain. After recovering enough to get clearance from his doctors to participate, he came into the third game of the season for a dozen or so plays only to be benched. He was furious. He had spent countless hours rehabilitating his injury and honing his skills in order to help the team win, yet he felt like the coaches did not appreciate his efforts. The coaches had not given him a chance to show what he could do.

At the next practice the offensive coordinator explained. He said, "Joey, you're my guy. You are our best drop-back passer. You know the game, understand our offense, and are exceptionally accurate. The problem isn't you, it's the offensive line. Until we can get that shored up, I have to go with someone who is more mobile. That knee brace is slowing you down too much." This thirty second explanation completely changed Joey's perspective. He went from railing against his situation to rallying to work even harder on his speed and agility.

The coach was unable to take the time in the heat of the game to explain why he pulled Joey from the field; however at the next opportunity he made his decision clear. A few words can make a big difference. Be conscious of how you interact with your team, your students. Are you recognizing the right behaviors and actions, both good and bad?

Are you linking the recognition to specific actions or behaviors that support your organization's goals and values? Things that you might consider recognizing include problem solving, getting out front of issues, leadership, ethical behaviors (especially in tough circumstances), motivating/inspiring others, committed team efforts, and going above and beyond to further organizational goals or support the growth of those you affect with your decisions. According to exit interviews, one of the primary reasons that people leave organizations is lack of recognition for their contributions. Bad management plays a huge role as well. Clearly those two factors go hand-in-glove.

Some folks are more motivated by a challenging assignment than they ever would be from a cash award. Acknowledgement can be anything from a kind word to a letter to framed artwork to stock options. It's not the recognition so much as how and when you do it that matters. Like goal setting, recognition should be SMART. Yes, we're using that acronym again, but this time the five elements stand for (1) Sincere, (2) Meaningful, (3) Adaptable, (4) Relevant, and (5) Timely. Here's how it works:

1. **Sincere**: this is sort of self-explanatory, but even sincere recognition can seem disingenuous if you don't do it right. Be specific about the behaviors or results that you value rather than offering generalized praise. Explain what was done, why it matters, and how much it means to you that the person did it.
2. **Meaningful**: any award should enhance the recognition, not be the recognition. Recognize others by showing respect, asking for input, giving feedback, providing opportunities, or just saying "thank you." Consider who and how to deliver the acknowledgement so that it will have the most meaning and impact. In hierarchical organizations, for instance, formal recognition events can provide career-affirming "face time" with key decision makers. Personalization makes it more meaningful too. For example, one of the most significant recognition items that Kane ever received was a handmade plaque that a program manager built in his shop and gave out to a handful of individuals who were instrumental in making the project a success. It was built from perhaps $3 or $4

worth of materials, but the inspiration upon receiving it was priceless because recipients responded to the thoughtfulness of the program manager's personal touch.
3. **Adaptable**: different people like to be recognized in different ways. For some a public event is embarrassing whereas others cherish the attention. Some people would be thrilled to receive football tickets, while others might prefer to attend the movies, an opera, or dinner theater. The better you know your team the better you can reward them in ways they will find meaningful and the better you can deliver appropriate recognition in alignment with individual predilections such as a preference for public or private recognition.
4. **Relevant**: keep the recognition appropriate in size for the achievement. Awarding 10,000 shares of stock for performing a routine job assignment is inappropriate, we all know that, but sometimes it is hard to directly tie recognition to the organizational impact of a person's actions. Don't overthink it; simply assure that every individual feels valued for their contributions, recognition is relevant with accomplishments, and that you are consistent in how and when you demonstrate appreciation to the team.
5. **Timely**: this may seem like a no-brainer, but if you work in a large organization it can take forethought and proactive action in order to work through the bureaucracy and receive approval to recognize employees in timely manner. Incorporate recognition planning into your operating rhythm so that you are always on the lookout for meritorious behaviors and have mechanisms in place to suitably recognize them in a timely manner.

That's all positive recognition. Don't forget about handling poor performance as well. Clearly you do not want to publically embarrass or diminish anyone, save in very, very rare circumstances, but oftentimes escapes can become learning moments, opportunities to improve processes, tools, or policies, or to send a powerful message about appropriate and inappropriate behaviors to the team. Don't let things slide. Hold everyone to established standards of performance, recognizing laudable behaviors and correcting inappropriate ones in a timely manner.

Above all, be consistent! If you appear to be playing favorites the recognition effort will backfire. Often spectacularly. Never forget that team members talk to each other. If you are not fair, objective, and consistent in how you apply recognition they will know. Few things undermine team cohesion and morale more than favoritism.

As you think about others, do not forget about recognizing yourself. This isn't about self-aggrandizement, but rather about maintaining your mental and physical health and well-being. Burn-out can be overlooked by self-starters, folks who have an overdeveloped sense of responsibility hence put their organization or team ahead of their own self-interests. They might start feeling the indicators of burn-out but ignore them to their detriment. Some of the warning signs include:

- **Cynicism**: you find yourself becoming pessimistic, always looking for the negatives in any situation. A famous radio personality once told Wilder, "Nobody wants to hear if a DJ had a bad day. If they keep bringing it up, nobody will hear about it because that DJ will be out of a job." Cynicism is poison to others; they will distance themselves from you and your organization if it persists.
- **Low energy**: you are dragging yourself to meet your goals. Often achievers will attribute this to their own failure(s). They will pump themselves up, mentally beat themselves up, and do whatever it takes to handle what they see as their shortcomings. Low energy is not always a function of poor health or bad nutrition; it can come from emotional drainage too. If you are experiencing low energy you may be having to allocate too much of your emotional energy to a turbulent teen, a demanding boss, a deep family problem, divorce, death, or some other energy sap internal or external to your organization.
- **Quick to anger**: if you find that you are uncharacteristically quick to anger pay attention. It's hard to be around folks

who lack patience and have a short fuse. If the situation continues it will create distance between you and those around you. Audit yourself and ask, "At what point did I start to become so angry?" Find that point and address how you can work around it to alleviate the emotion. You may find that incident is where the burnout began.
- **Self-medication**: some people reach for assistance beyond a cup of coffee or Red Bull® to get up and get tasks done. If alcohol or drugs have become a crutch, you have a problem with burnout *and* drugs. That's a very bad combination. Seek professional help; you are not living the life you are meant to live. We mean it.
- **Hunger and cravings**: we all get them, but are you using certain foods to help your body feel better in the short term? Look to fats, salts, and sugars. If you are using foods high in these contents you might be experiencing burnout but making your body feel safe and warm by giving it abnormally large doses of what it naturally craves.
- **Sleep**: sleep too much or too little due to anxiety or depression. Significant changes in sleep patterns or reliance on over-the-counter drugs to experience normal sleep may be indicators of serious problems. If you experience sustained changes in your natural rhythm check with a medical professional.
- **Pains**: if you are having aches and pains in your body that are hard to explain, such as persistent headaches or backaches, this can be your body telling you that it is reaching a breakpoint. Oftentimes this is nature forcing you to slow down and audit your place in the world. Heed the warning, slow down, and take a hard look before it becomes a serious situation requiring medical attention.

If you are experiencing one or more of these symptoms examine your life to find the root cause. It may be necessary to seek medical treatment, but oftentimes something as simple as a vacation and conscious attitude adjustment will resolve the issue. Since many members of your team may crave more challenging assignments, delegating effectively may be one of those "two birds; one stone" things that really helps.

Sensei, Mentor, Teacher, Coach Tip:

> Corkboard it. The metaphor of a corkboard, a public acknowledgement of others' works, is a great thing to do. When somebody takes the time to do something, whether it is building ships in a bottle or working at the local teen center, they have chosen to spend their life energy doing something that brings them satisfaction. It is important as a leader to acknowledge positive activities that are outside your influence. This makes your team members' lives bigger. It acknowledges their value, what they choose to do with their lives, and makes a statement that you as a leader have taken initiative to shine a spotlight on them and their work. Oftentimes this is done during a staff meeting or via an organizational website or newsletter.

Action:

Sincere, meaningful, adaptable, relevant, and timely recognition is motivational, but more importantly it's the right thing to do. The challenge is that leaders who have not developed a mindset of continuously looking for opportunities to recognize others tend to get caught up in concerns of the day and never get around to doing it.

Do you manage your calendar using Outlook or a similar program? If so, add a new meeting notice, one that recurs at least once a week, reminding yourself to look for opportunities to recognize members of your team. If not, make a mental note to be on the lookout for actions that are instrumental to your organization's success. You may or may not find accomplishments worthy of formal recognition on a daily or weekly basis, projects often take time to complete, but if you have a solid team you should spot behaviors worth reinforcing all the time.

Some folks are naturally great at making those around them feel appreciated; others not so much. Look at other leaders in your organization who excel at recognition to find examples that you can emulate. Also consider books like *Love 'Em or Lose 'Em: Getting Good*

People to Stay by Beverly Kaye and Sharon Jordan-Evans, *Make Their Day: Employee Recognition That Works* by Cindy Ventrice, or *365 Ways to Motivate and Reward Your Employees Every Day: With Little or No Money* by Dianna Podmoroff for inspiration.

Sensei, Mentor, Teacher, Coach – Little Life Secret:

> The things we dislike in others are oftentimes the very things we have within ourselves. Find out if that is true. If it is, take action to fix that trait immediately.

18

MORE THAN JUST TECHNIQUES

Assuring Strategic Alignment

Policy:

> "If words of command are not clear and distinct, if orders are not thoroughly understood, then the general is to blame. But, if orders are clear and the soldiers nevertheless disobey, then it is the fault of their officers."
> Sun Tzu[34]

Application:

> "Tell them what you are going to tell them, tell them, and then tell them what you told them."
> Paul White[35]

The tin man stopped at the edge of the field, the rattling of his merchandise signaling to the farmer that he had items for sale. In need of a new pot for his wife, the farmer crossed his newly turned field to meet the smiling tin man.

"What can I show you my fine friend?"

"Dunno just yet, let me see yer wares." The farmer paused a short distance from the cart, squinting in the afternoon sun. He pointed to a pot he thought might replace the dilapidated one in his home. "How much?"

After bargaining it was agreed, one quarter of a coin and some freshly baked bread. The farmer called to his son who was working nearby and told the young man, "Go ta the house n' tell your mother I have bought a pan for her. Bring me one quarter coin and bread."

The farmer's son ran to the nearby dwelling and returned with what his father had requested. As the exchange was made the tin man inquired about another small hut in the distance, "Would that household be interested in some of my wares?"

"They have many burdens and no money. They have no son. He was lost to highwaymen." The Farmer pointed to his son's arm where a jagged scar was present, "My son, he survives because he knows how to fight. I taught him well."

This story illustrates how the eldest son had learned the family's fighting method. It may have been simple, perhaps it was complex, but what really matters is that it was effective. That family still had access to one of its greatest resources, work that could be performed by their oldest son. The family across the way, on the other hand, was deprived not only of their son's labor, but also that of his probable offspring.

Throughout most of human history life was difficult. City states rather than nations were the dominant form of government. There were social norms but, depending on the time period and location, few if any laws and no police to enforce them. For much of history most folks had to fend for themselves. With no social safety net, the only thing a person could rely on was his or her family, most of whom tended to die young of malnutrition, injury, or illness. Those with strength of arms, numbers, or superior equipment rode roughshod over their less fortunate neighbors. Consequently fighting skills were vital for pretty much everyone, from peasant to prince, and the process of acquiring them was serious indeed. Those forms of training were brutal and effective, but are simply not suitable for the modern citizen today. We cannot train people in the classical manner.

Ask anybody who has been practicing martial arts for thirty years or more about their early training and they will tell you how difficult and severe it was, oftentimes abusive and extreme. The origins of that environment began much earlier, oftentimes hundreds of years earlier, and went with the needs of the time.

When the ancient masters developed their art forms they lived during a period where they not only had to fend for themselves but during which just about any injury suffered at the hands of an adversary would mean that the victim would become incapacitated and/or die of infection or starvation. Fights that could not be avoided were short and brutal, leaving cripples and corpses behind. Instructional methods designed for that pitiless period remained much the same despite the fact that the reasons behind them had changed (in much of the developed world, anyway).

We asked a United States Marine a very simple question, "Was your drill instructor hard on you?" Unsurprisingly he answered, "Yes." The follow up question shifted the timeline a little, "When you were getting ready to finish basic training did your drill instructor hate you?" His answer, again in straightforward Marine fashion was, "No."

There are many reasons drill instructors are hard on their recruits, first and foremost because if they do their jobs properly the recruits are more likely to survive when they are deployed on the battlefield. A soldier's job, after all, is to kill people, break things, and blow stuff up when fighting an enemy who is doing their level best to do the same nasty things to them. Marine Corps training is hard, austere, and purposely difficult because Marines are likely to be on the front lines whenever we find ourselves in war.

The fictional farmer's son had a similar experience. He had to be ready to defend himself against raiders, brigands, and thugs at a moment's notice, knowing that any slip would be his last. He could not count on assistance from law enforcement or enjoy the benefits of modern medicine. Injuries that proved fatal in the farmer's time, even those that were deadly as recently as a quarter century ago, are survivable today.

We practice far more than we fight. Not only are fights uncommon in modern society, but long fights are exceedingly rare. In movies we might glory at long, drawn out battles with artfully choreographed movements, but real life altercations lasting more than a few seconds simply do not happen when people are doing their level best to hurt each other. In fact, 15 to 20 seconds is exceptionally long.

To even give this a better perspective let's do a little math. Each day is made up of 86,400 seconds, so a 15 second fight takes up 0.00017 percent of your day. Fifteen seconds is an intense seventeen thousandths of a day to be sure, but it is still an infinitesimal amount of time. To average that over the amount of your lifetime, well the number would be so ridiculously small that we are not even going to indulge in the math. In comparison, martial artists might average a handful of hours a week practicing. Breaking that down, if you spend four hours a week on the *dojo* floor that adds up to an average of about 2,000 seconds a day, a massive 0.023 percent of your time.

It is preposterous to discuss the viability of fighting as much as you train. Most of life is practice. If you're in the military you drill more than you fight. If you are a professional athlete you practice more than you play. Even in business, chances are good that you spend a lot of your time in meetings, travel, training, and other activities that help assure your skills remain up to speed rather than performing work on the products or services that your company sells.

The intensity of a fight is extraordinary, the execution intense, the moment small. Fighting is the black hole of human existence, deep, dark, and dense. Winners and losers are made in practice. We have all heard, "You play like you practice," "Train hard; fight easy," "Sweat when you train or bleed when you fight," or some variation along that theme. It's true, yet you can also have "puncher's luck," a maxim in boxing circles that means if you keep throwing punches something good might happen.

The challenge with training is that in order to be able to put it into application you must understand more than just techniques. You need to know the strategy as well. Every martial system contains both a strategy, which may be hidden, as well as tactics that can readily be found in the style's forms or applications. Strategy is a plan of action. In martial arts as in war, it is what you do to prepare for engagement with an enemy long before the fight begins. Tactics, on the other hand, are expedient means of achieving an end, in this case defeating an adversary. Tactics are the applications that you see (or decipher), while strategy is the overarching plan that ties them together into a cohesive whole.

Looking at how frequently techniques come up in the various core forms of a classical martial system (e.g., karate, *taekwondo*, *kung fu*) can be a good way to ascertain its strategy. Look for patterns that are repeated within and between the various *kata* (forms). Tactics are selected during the heat of battle, yet without strategy they will ultimately fail. The tactics of every combat art were developed within a strategic framework that allows them to work effectively.

Tactical thinking is based around the concept of "if"—"If he does this, I will do that." The challenge is that you simply cannot think of enough ifs to anticipate every conceivable situation. When faced with an unexpected movement during actual combat, your brain will freeze, if only for a brief moment, rendering you temporarily defenseless and vulnerable. If the strategic foundation is strong, on the other hand, appropriate tactics can be employed automatically without much if any conscious thought, letting you react appropriately to most any situation without hesitating.

A deep understanding of strategy, therefore, is a necessary prerequisite for being able to make the most of any martial art. There are simply too many techniques to apply without knowing the context in which they work most effectively. While most arts cover the entire gamut of punching, kicking, throwing, choking, pressure points, and whatnot to some degree, every art excels at certain areas to the detriment of others. You simply cannot be the best at everything. Karate, for example, is primarily a striking art while judo is primarily a grappling style. Both are effective and both share many of the same tactics, yet their strategies are different.

Warrior arts throughout history have been built around solid strategic foundations. For example, by the height of their empire, Rome's legions (*legio*) had conquered much of the known world. A large reason for their amazing success was a solid strategy on which everything else was built. The core of that strategy was, at its most basic level, based on discipline and unity.

Professional foot soldiers formed the vast majority of the Roman army at that time. These soldiers trained specifically for close-quarters combat. Though the exact formation and structure of the legions varied depending upon the time period one examines, each division of soldiers—century (~ 80 men), cohort (~ 480 men), and legion (~ 5,240 men)—had its own battle standard. Though used primarily to facilitate command and communication, battle standards also helped to preserve the cohesiveness and pride of each unit, as they represented a concrete symbol of that unit's achievements and were also used in various religious rituals designed to promote unity. The most important standard in each legion was the legionary eagle made of a precious metal (usually silver), a potent symbol of the power of Rome and the honor of the legion. In wartime, officers called standard-bearers (*signifer*) held these battle standards. These individuals stood out from other soldiers by the animal-head skins they wore.

Just as the military structure of the legion was designed to promote discipline and unity, so too was the equipment the troops were issued and tactics they deployed. Each foot soldier was given a very short thrusting sword (*gladius*), a large shield (*scutum*), a couple of javelins (*pila*), and at least minimal armor (covering much of the head, torso, forearms, and shins). When fighting, they threw their *pila* to disrupt an enemy, picking off easy targets, and then closed ranks to engage in carefully orchestrated hand-to-hand combat. In close-quarters range, they were trained to attack the nearest enemy soldier diagonally across from them, thrusting through the small gaps between their interlocked shields. Roman soldiers almost never aimed for an enemy combatant directly in front of them, relying instead on their fellow warriors to handle that threat.

These short swords and interlocking shields forced the Romans to work together as a unit, each soldier protecting the other. Individual fighting ability counted far less than organization and coordination. They methodically moved forward as a disciplined unit, decimating and trampling their less organized foe. In this manner, everything in the military structure, equipment, training, and tactics all reinforced the Romans' overall strategy.

Strategy works the same way in the martial arts. Everything from stances to breathing, including movement, striking, kicking, grappling, and defensive postures, are all directly tied to a system's strategy. It is holistic, self-contained, and unique to every art. Sports teams work the same way, as do businesses. Any successful organization must have a sound strategy backed up by a set of viable tactics that can assure implementation. Training those tactics while keeping their strategic foundation in mind is a recipe for success.

Like ripples from a pebble tossed into a pond, decisions you make can have far reaching collateral blights or benefits. Strategic thinkers are aware of potential consequences or implications of judgments they make. It is vital to rise up above the daily minutia and keep your organization or team's strategy firmly in mind as you implement plans, projects, tactics and techniques. For example, there are three primary ways that organizations differentiate themselves from their competitors:

1. **Operational excellence** (e.g., UPS, Dell): providing customers with reliable products or services at competitive prices that are delivered with minimal inconvenience. Continuously improving efficiencies to drive profit margins.
2. **Customer intimacy** (e.g., Nordstrom, Home Depot): precisely segmenting and targeting markets, then tailoring offerings to exactly match the demands of customers in each niche. Combining this detailed customer knowledge with the flexibility to respond quickly to almost any need.
3. **Product differentiation** (e.g., Apple, Nike): offering customers leading-edge products or services that consistently enhance the customer's use of the merchandise. Understanding what their customers value and boosting the level they come to expect beyond what competitors can provide.

In their article "Customer Intimacy and Other Value Disciplines," published in January, 1993 in the *Harvard Business Review*, Michael

Treacy and Fred Wiersema stated:

> *"Companies that pursue the same value discipline have remarkable similarities, regardless of their industry... An employee could transfer from FedEx to Wal-Mart and, after getting oriented, feel right at home. Likewise, the systems, structures, and cultures of product leaders such as Johnson & Johnson in health care and pharmaceuticals and Nike in sport shoes look much like one another. But across two disciplines, the similarities end. Send people from Wal-Mart to Nike and they would think they were on a different planet."*

Just as you cannot be all things to all people, neither can your organization. While virtually all businesses have pockets of operational excellence, customer intimacy, and product differentiation, a strategic focus is necessary to assure that projects and priorities align with their primary focus area. Think back on the organizational mission and values statements we discussed in Chapter 11 and the SMART goals and objectives from Chapter 6. It is not only vital that these align, but also that you clearly communicate how they fit together for your team.

It is fairly self-evident on a sports team in many cases, but in a large institution it is easy to get caught up in the role you play and forget about the business you are in. If you are an IT architect, for example, the technology you work on is far less important than how it is used to support the products or services that keep your company in business.

So, how does this work in real life? An organization that excels at the customer intimacy model is Starbucks. The company is a great example of a well thought out business plan taken to fruition. Inspired by the espresso bars in Milan, Italy, Howard Schultz wanted to introduce the European coffee bar culture to America, so he opened their first location in Seattle's Pike Place Market in 1971. Today Starbucks has over 7,500 locations in over 30 different countries.

Their mission, "To inspire and nurture the human spirit—one person, one cup and one neighborhood at a time," offers insight into their corporate strategy. The term "inspire and nurture" is largely about market segmentation; rather than simply selling beverages, they strive to deliver an experience, one that has customers gladly paying $5.00 for what would otherwise be a fifty cent cup of coffee. This strategy plays throughout the vision and principles the company instills upon its employees:

- ***Our coffee:*** *it has always been, and will always be, about quality. We're passionate about ethically sourcing the finest coffee beans, roasting them with great care, and improving the lives of people who grow them. We care deeply about all of this; our work is never done.*
- ***Our partners:*** *we're called partners, because it's not just a job, it's our passion. Together, we embrace diversity to create a place where each of us can be ourselves. We always treat each other with respect and dignity. And we hold each other to that standard.*
- ***Our customers:*** *when we are fully engaged, we connect with, laugh with, and uplift the lives of our customers—even if just for a few moments. Sure, it starts with the promise of a perfectly made beverage, but our work goes far beyond that. It's really about human connection.*
- ***Our stores:*** *when our customers feel this sense of belonging, our stores become a haven, a break from the worries outside, a place where you can meet with friends. It's about enjoyment at the speed of life—sometimes slow and savored, sometimes faster. Always full of humanity.*
- ***Our neighborhood:*** *every store is part of a community, and we take our responsibility to be good neighbors seriously. We want to be invited in wherever we do business. We can be a force for positive action—bringing together our partners, customers, and the community to contribute every day. Now we see that our responsibility—and our potential for good—is even larger. The world is looking to Starbucks to set the new standard, yet again. We will lead.*
- ***Our shareholders:*** *we know that as we deliver in each of these areas, we enjoy the kind of success that rewards our shareholders. We are fully accountable to get each of these elements right so that Starbucks—and everyone it touches—can endure and thrive.*

Powerful words, huh? Starbucks' corporate strategy of delivering an experience rather than just a product shines through, particularly in phrases like, "It's our passion," "We uplift the lives of our customers," "Our stores become a haven," "Feel this sense of belonging," and "Enjoyment at the speed of life." This is the classic customer intimacy model made real.

Taking it a step further, CFO Troy Alstead reported on CNN that twenty five percent of all their transactions are pre-paid via Starbucks gift cards or mobile payment technology applications. When customer loyalty programs are added into the mix, fully one third of all transactions at Starbucks are pre-paid. That's simultaneously a significant measure of brand loyalty as well as a healthy and predictable source of revenue.

Starbucks formed a partnership with Apple to collaborate on offering music and computer content as part of their coffeehouse experience, giving away complimentary "song of the week" and "application of the week" downloads. Free Wi-Fi, couches, fireplaces, and the like help turn many of their stores into "destinations," one of many ways they differentiate themselves from run-of-the-mill fast food joints.

Even in overseas locations, this customer experience is largely the same. American tourists feel right at home, yet so do the locals who have bought in to the Starbucks culture. To help assure continuity of vision and align motivation throughout their employee base, they offer stock awards and often promote from within, factors that helped them earn a spot in Fortune magazine's list of top 100 companies to work for in 2013.

While Starbucks is primarily known for selling coffee, they also peddle other hot and cold beverages, pastries, sandwiches, candy, and snacks. Regardless, the layout of the stores, branding, merchandising, customer interactions, and so on all play a role in fulfilling the strategy of delivering an experience rather than a product or service. What they sell, what they do, what they are, all the tactics are tied to that overarching strategy.

Sensei, Mentor, Teacher, Coach Tip:

> A strategy is a long-term plan of action designed to achieve a particular goal. Tactics, on the other hand, are expedient means of achieving an end. Like a house without a solid foundation, tactics without strategy will ultimately fail. Even as the Roman's strategy rippled throughout their entire military infrastructure, so too should your team or organization's strategy be aligned to assure that you can achieve your goals.

Action:

Examine the linkage between your organization's mission and vision, and your individual goals and objectives. Like the structure of the Roman legions or implementation of the Starbucks' business plan, there should be clear ties between the strategic goals and tactical action plans. One way to do that in large organizations is a "you are here" exercise. Start with the top level mission, vision, and objectives, and draw a picture that drills all the way down to your area.

Everyone in your group should easily be able to identify how they support the enterprise. There should be an obvious linkage clarifying how every project or task you work on a daily basis supports the higher-level priorities, products, and services delivered. If you cannot find one start asking questions. It may be time for a change.

Sensei, Mentor, Teacher, Coach – Little Life Secret:

> Strategic thinking has been a vital aspect of leadership since ancient times. In fact, the word strategy comes from the Greek word strategos, a title reserved for military commanders in the Athenian army.

19

DOING THE RIGHT THING

Ethics and Morals to Live and Be Remembered By

"Leadership is solving problems. The day soldiers stop bringing you their problems is the day you have stopped leading them. They have either lost confidence that you can help or concluded you do not care. Either case is a failure of leadership."
Colin Powell[36]

Field of Dreams is a classic baseball movie. Even those who don't enjoy the sport can find value in the film's message. Here is a short scene in which Ray has built a baseball field on his farm and the ghosts of history's greatest ballplayers have walked out of the adjacent cornfield to greet him:

> Ray Kinsella: *"Where'd they come from?"*
>
> Shoeless Joe Jackson: *"Where did WE come from? You wouldn't believe how many guys wanted to play here. We had to beat 'em off with a stick."*
>
> Archie Graham: *"Hey, that's Smokey Joe Wood. And Mel Ott. And Gil Hodges!"*
>
> Shoeless Joe Jackson: *"Ty Cobb wanted to play, but none of us could stand the son-of-a-bitch when we were alive, so we told him to stick it!"*

Ty Cobb was an incredible baseball player. He played his last game in 1928 and was inducted into the MLB Hall of Fame in 1936, yet he is still an undeniable leader in the world of baseball statistics today. At .367, Cobb still has the highest batting average of all time. In fact, after his rookie year he never hit below .300 during a season. His other records include 2,246 runs scored (2nd all time), 4,191 hits (2nd all time), 723 doubles (4th all time), 297 triples (2nd all time), 1,938 RBIs (6th all time), and 892 stolen bases (4th all time).

Yes, Ty Cobb was a phenomenal baseball player. But, he was also a nasty human being. He fought both on and off the field with other players, fans, and even umpires. For example, in 1907 during spring training in Augusta, Georgia, a groundskeeper named Bungy attempted to pat Cobb on the shoulder (or possibly shake his hand, reports vary). The overly familiar greeting infuriated Cobb who viciously attacked. When Bungy's wife tried to defend him, Cobb choked her. The assault was finally stopped when catcher Charles "Boss" Schmidt intervened, knocking Cobb out. Cobb clearly knew how he was perceived, but appeared not to care, writing, "In legend I am a sadistic, slashing, swashbuckling despot who waged war in the guise of sport."

Don't be Ty Cobb. Don't build a dirty legacy.

In today's world students, fans, and athletes oftentimes get a pass, at least in the media… leaders don't, period. And since you are a leader you don't get a pass, a second chance, a do-over. Players and students get treated differently than you do. As a *sensei*, mentor, teacher, or coach you are held, and should hold yourself, to a different standard. Your actions are noted by your team and they will follow your example, even if it's a bad one.

Here is an example: In 2004 Canadian Football League kicker Paul McCallum missed a field goal that would have given the Saskatchewan Roughriders football team an overtime victory over the B.C. Lions in the Western Conference Championship. McCallum's home was egged within an hour of the end of the game. Shortly thereafter a truck pulled up and, in front of his wife who was still in the process of cleaning up the egg mess, backed up and dumped a load of manure on his lawn.

How would it sit in your mind if the manure had been dumped onto the McCallum family lawn by McCallum's head coach instead of by an outraged fan? Would the coach have a job in the morning? The answer is clearly no. We would all be mortified to hear that any coach would pull such an immature and damaging stunt. Yet it is likely (we were not able to confirm what happened post incident) that the person who dumped the manure got at worst some form of a small civil fine and returned to work the following Monday morning.

Leaders should always be held to a higher standard. Even in politics…

You may have heard that in 1999, then Vice President of the United States Dick Cheney broke the law when he picked up the phone at his desk inside the White House and made calls to deep-pocket contributors soliciting money for the Republican National Committee, the political arm of the then sitting administration. Section 607 of Title 18 of the U.S. Criminal Code clearly states there is to be no solicitation of campaign funds in federal government offices, yet Vice President Cheney had done just that. He had violated the statute as it was clearly and succinctly written.

In fact that particular law is so clear that members of Congress regularly leave the capital building and go out to the parking lot to make campaign calls since that area is not considered a "federal office." When Cheney was caught, his defense was that the law had never been tested in court. Consequently there was no precedence, rendering the law just a theory. If the law is just a theory went his reasoning, then there was no real control, therefore he had broken no rules.

You have heard that, right?

In reality this event actually happened in 1997. It was not Vice President Cheney but rather Vice President Al Gore who, upon getting caught, uttered the now famous phrase, "There is no controlling legal authority that says this was in violation of law." He stated this during his March 3, 1997 press conference where he addressed the accusations.

Yes, Vice President Gore broke the law as it was written, and as everybody understood it was supposed to be interpreted, yet his defense was in essence, "There is no case law, so if you want to come get me, well, feel free. That is going to take a while. It is also going to be very expensive. As a sitting Vice President I have a bully pulpit and government-paid attorneys, all willing to prove that I was not wrong, but not right either. Further, there is no money in this for you. So, what are you going to do now?"

Oftentimes people spin "right" or "wrong" into whether or not they agree with the person who did it, perhaps thinking that the ends justifies the means regardless of ethics, morals, or laws. That is why we changed the people and the parties—to show that it makes no difference who made the illegal phone solicitations. This practice is distasteful regardless. While many issues have shades of grey, leaders must draw ethical boundaries for themselves; codes of behavior that chart their moral compasses.

Roughly 2,500 years ago the Greek philosopher Heraclitus of Ephesus wrote words that still resonate today:

> *"The soul is dyed the color of its thoughts. Think only on those things that are in line with your principles and can bear the full light of day. The content of your character is your choice. Day by day, what you choose, what you think, and what you do is who you become. Your integrity is your destiny… it is the light that guides your way."*

Integrity is sometimes defined as doing the right thing even when no one is watching. Without integrity it is virtually impossible to be a leader. Three things that leaders *do not* do are belief perseverance, illusory correlation, and regression to the mean.

1. **Belief perseverance**: the act of adhering to a belief when the facts indicate otherwise. An example is in the story above. Did you find a way to justify your preconceived notions of the people involved based upon your political affiliation? Did you let your prejudices cloud your position, thinking something like, "There has to be more to the story," in order to meet your mental constructs? This is non-

rational. Leaders do not engage in belief perseverance. When the information is still incomplete or unable to be confirmed, well that leaves the issue open, but when leaders uncover facts that counter long held opinions they are willing to change their minds. The phrase, "We make decisions based on facts and data," resonates for just that reason.

2. **Illusory correlation**: is the process of seeing a relationship, a linking between variables that does not exist. Look at this way, what if a friend told you, "Every time I eat black licorice, my favorite sports team wins." There could be a correlation, but clearly there is no causation. What your friend eats has absolutely nothing to do with his team or their performance on the field. This is the domain of the conspiracy theorist, not the realm of a leader.

3. **Regression to the mean**: is a term used in statistics to demonstrate the fact that when you measure an extreme at one end of a spectrum and compare it with an extreme at the other end the two will adjust, moving toward the middle. If you own an indexed fund such as the S&P 500 or Russell 2000, you are spreading your investments across a representative sampling of the "market," reducing your downside risk and upside opportunity as the various stocks tend to balance each other out. This allows for slow, steady movement whereas if you had invested in a single stock (or handful of them) you could expect wild fluctuations over time. Regression to the mean might be useful for investing, but you are not average. You are not a regression to the mean. The mean is mediocrity. People need to be able to look to their leaders and know their value immediately. Leaders strive for more than average and in doing so they do the right things to get there.

Leaders must do the right thing even when the choices are very difficult, even when there is no good or right option to select. If you are a science fiction fan, you have undoubtedly heard of the *Kobayashi Maru*. For those unfamiliar, it was a no-win scenario given as a character test to prospective officers in the fictional Star Trek universe.

The set-up was a mission to rescue a civilian vessel, the *Kobayashi Maru*, which was stranded in the neutral zone between the militant Klingon Empire (the bad guys) and Federation (the good guys) space. The approaching cadet crew had to decide whether to attempt a rescue, endangering their ship and potentially sparking an interstellar war, or leave the civilian vessel to its fate (near certain destruction). The hero, James T. Kirk, hacks into the computer and reprograms the scenario so that he can rescue the stranded ship without getting himself and his crew killed in the process.

Sometimes you can "cheat" like Kirk, using creativity or innovation to find a good way out of a "no-win" situation, but more often than not that simply isn't the case. There is no good thing to do, only the right thing to do. Even when you would much rather ignore it and hope that it will go away or pawn it off on somebody else, it is vital to remember that making tough decisions comes with the territory. Ignoring brewing problems, abdicating responsibility, or attempting to cover up messes that should have been prevented tends to end badly.

Failing to do the right thing in tough situations tends to not only torpedo the careers of those involved, but also harms their organizations as well. Consider the case of former Penn State assistant football coach Jerry Sandusky who was convicted of using his position with the team to abuse children and sentenced to 30 to 60 years in prison for his crimes (which he is attempting to appeal). Three former Penn State administrators (President Graham Spanier, vice president Gary Schultz, and athletic director Tim Curley) who allegedly knew of this behavior yet failed to act await trial on charges they engaged in a criminal cover-up of the scandal. The situation led to the departure of iconic football coach Joe Paterno, damaged his reputation, and cost the university well over $100M, including a settlement of $59.7M to 26 men who said they were sexually abused as children and over $50 million on other costs such as lawyers' fees, public relations expenses, and adoption of new policies and procedures to prevent reoccurrences. Regardless of the outcome of their trial, the reputations of the university and the men involved will be forever tarnished.

So, what to do about it? Consider these six things:

1. **Give more than others expect**: the example you set is what others will emulate. When you set the right tone, put in the hard work, and communicate effectively, doing the right thing can become pervasive throughout the organization. Just like star players have a habit of arriving early and staying late, so do successful coaches, teachers, and businesspeople.
2. **Expect more from others**: setting high expectations for yourself and others is always important, but never more so than when it comes to ethics and culture. This must include the reward structure as well. For example, The Boeing Company uses a set of leadership attributes to grade its managers, affecting all aspects of their compensation, retention, and promote-ability. One of these measures is, "Lives the Boeing values." This means that it is unacceptable to deliver results through unethical, abusive, or deceptive practices, helping assure that the company's leadership at all levels throughout the organization is incentivized to do the right things.
3. **Consider public opinion**: think about how the situation might look if it were on the front page of *The Wall Street Journal*, and then do the right thing in the eyes of the public. This gets back to Heraclitus's admonishment about bearing the "full light of day." Understand and respond to stakeholders' perceptions and expectations for you and your organization.
4. **Own the problem**: few things frustrate stakeholders more than obfuscation. You've probably heard the terms "weasel-wording" or "lawyering-up." That is a really good way to lose friends and discourage people. Step up and do what is necessary to make things right. Done properly, the goodwill you generate can far exceed the cost.
5. **Take action**: talking is not enough; issues are managed with communication but resolved through actions. No one will believe you if they do not see concrete accomplishments and corrective actions. In fact, the way you handle a

problem will oftentimes be remembered far longer than the crisis itself. For example, it is customary for restaurants to comp meals whenever an entrée is cooked incorrectly, say a medium-well steak when medium-rare was ordered, even if it is due to a customer's misconception of what 'correct' should be. They do this because the practice engenders consumer loyalty.

6. **Contain quickly**: this is a crisis-communication principle. If something looks like it is out of control and has the potential of going viral (e.g., the Sandusky scandal) it is vital to anticipate and get ahead of events. Doing the right thing alone may not be enough if you are generating headline news. In fact, if it gets to that point you will likely need to hire a professional to help you navigate the damage control process. Even when the crisis is no longer in the headlines that does not necessarily mean that it is has been forgotten. Remember the Exxon Valdez oil spill? That incident took place in 1989.

It can be tough to do the right thing for several reasons. To begin, you need sufficient understanding of the situation and moral clarity to figure out what "right" means in the first place. Beyond that, you need the fortitude to make tough decisions even when they may personally impact you and those you care about. Nevertheless, that's exactly what leaders do.

Sensei, Mentor, Teacher, Coach Tip:

> Most people have a pretty good moral compass. Consequently, once you understand a situation knowing the right thing is easy. While doing the right thing can be hard, it tends to get easier when you consider how your actions might look from an outsider's perspective. If you wouldn't mind seeing your story on the front page of *The Wall Street Journal* or some other prestigious national periodical, you're probably on the right track.

Doing the Right Thing

Action:

In the 1984 movie *Starman*, Jeff Bridges plays a human-looking alien who has come to earth. He learns to blend in by emulating other people's actions. After observing how people drive he comes to the conclusion that, "Red means stop, green means go, yellow means go faster." It's funny in the movies, but makes an important point about real life as well. Laws are nothing more than ideas put on paper if people don't follow them. For example, most folks have committed violations for speeding, jaywalking, and littering, amongst a host of other "small" things that didn't seem all that important at the time. Are you one of them? If so, would you do the same thing if your child was watching? What about if you were on a reality TV show with a national audience?

Doing the right thing begins by expecting more of yourself. Look back to Chapter 11 and your personal mission statement. If you have not created one, now is the time. If you already have, give it a read through and make sure that you have adequately addressed the ethics and morals you wish to live and be remembered by. Circumstances can overwhelm if you do not keep those principles firmly in mind.

Sensei, Mentor, Teacher, Coach – Little Life Secret:

> Perception oftentimes trumps reality. Facts and data alone make little difference if others are not convinced. Consequently you not only have to model the right behaviors consistently, but also help people see the change you are making. And, be patient. The process takes time.

PASSIO

Leadership for the Right Reasons

"The reward for being the best through hard work is not about you. It's not for you, it's for others. It's not about praise and adulation. There is only one guarantee for achieving the level of 'best' for all your hard work, for the hours of toiling in the weight room, for grinding it out on the field, and for helping carry your team to victory... more hard work to stay there. The true reward of being the best through hard work isn't you being better than others; it's you being better for others."
Coach Darin Slack[37]

The Latin word *passio* means suffering or sacrifice. It is also the root word of passion (as in the Passion of Christ), though we are using it here without any religious affiliation. Anyone who is a parent may not recognize the term, yet they are intimately familiar with the concept whenever they put their child's interests ahead of their own. What responsible parent has not stayed up late to care for a sick child, help with homework, or offer a shoulder to cry on?

Yes, parents are familiar with the concept, but effective leaders are too. Most of us put others ahead of ourselves, often more frequently than we are willing to admit. We are willing to sacrifice our time, our resources, our emotional well-being, and in some cases even our lives for the things we care about—our country, our organization, our fraternity or sorority, our religion, our team, etc. In serving others we, without exception, find merit in ourselves, our purpose, and our relationship with the rest of humanity. It's not just about going out of our way to do a good dead, contribute to charity, or lend a hand. Simply being there, listening, or offering a heartfelt word of encouragement can make a tremendous difference to those around us.

It's all in the attitude. If you're doing it solely for yourself people will know. They may not know today, they may not know tomorrow, but eventually they will come to see your stripes and it will be your undoing. Your actions will become suspect, all of them. No matter how well you think you can disguise it, selfishness is transparent. If your motivation is self-aggrandizement, self-centered, and designed for you, you are unlikely to succeed over the long term.

If you do it for the betterment of the group, people will know that too. Ambition certainly has its place, few folks are so altruistic that they do not want and expect reward for all their hard work and sacrifice. We are all disappointed if we put in the effort and it does not come to fruition. Nevertheless, the underpinnings of all that hard work need to be selfless, working toward the betterment of the team, the organization, or even the betterment of mankind.

In the fifth-century BC, Lao-Tzu wrote:

> *"The highest type of ruler is one of whose existence the people are barely aware… The sage is self-effacing and scanty of words. When his task is accomplished and things have been completed, all the people say, 'we ourselves have achieved it!'"*

That is the difference between a leader and a manager. You do not have to be in charge to lead, but you do need to set a good example. If you are always looking out for the welfare of those in your sphere of responsibility it's hard to go wrong.

Here's an exercise to help:

To advance along your leadership journey, you must be able to answer four questions with clarity: (1) What is your talent, (2) What makes you mad, (3) What did you love at the age of seven, and (4) Where does this lead you. Work fast, as overthinking puts you in your head and not in your heart. The heart works fast, the head… well that is a process. Work from your heart now. If you have already developed your personal mission statement in Chapter 11 this exercise should be easier. This may seem redundant, but the two drills go hand-in-glove, taking different tacks to provide greater clarity.

1. What is my talent?

You know you have a talent, likely more than one. Quickly, list them in no particular order; put whatever is top of mind first. Just go, now!

a) _____

b) _____

c) _____

2. What makes me mad?

One of the most common questions folks ask is what you like. If you enjoy doing something it often leads toward teaching, mentoring, or coaching others about it. But, this is not your first take for this exercise. You need to work in reverse order. Go to the opposite, determining what drives you crazy? What do you dislike? What agitates you? This process helps moves you away from what you dislike, driving clarity in where you need to go. List the top three things that make you mad here:

a) _____

b) _____

c) _____

3. What did I love at the age of seven?

Look back to your childhood. Specifically, focus your attention on what was important to you when you were about seven years old. That is the age when you began to grow your identity as an individual, started to separate from your parents who up until that time had been the center of everything in your life. This is the time period in which you are likely to find the igniter. Seek the activity where you lost track of time. Whatever lit your fire as a child likely carries over into adulthood, it is hardwired in most of us. Audit your childhood for your most joyful and fulfilling activities, behaviors, and things that you loved to do and list them here:

a) _____

b) _____

c) _____

4. Where does this lead me?

Now that you have the components, you can organize them in a meaningful way.

My talents are _____, _____, and _____. I want to avoid _____, _____, and _____, and I get lost in the activities of _____, _____, and _____.

Now, take some time to think about what you have just written and then fill in the following sentence:

The juice of my life is: _____, I love doing _____, and will avoid _____.

Now, knowing this, what does your life look like today? Are you living a life that jives with your self-vision? If it is not, why are you failing to leverage your talents, your desires, and your fire? Sure, any old job can pay the bills, but if you are going to spend half your life (or more) doing something to earn a living it ought not to feel too much like work. Most importantly, how are you using or going to use this path to ignite the fire in others? It is in using our gifts, our fire, in the benefit of others that we move from simply existing, to truly being human.

Sensei, Mentor, Teacher, Coach Tip:

> Take a moment to look back to the one person who found something in you that you did not know existed, a teacher, a mentor, or a coach. Look to how they were able to light your flame. They used their fire didn't they? Pay it forward. Don't try too hard to copy their methods, but do emulate their intent.

Action:

Between the exercise in this chapter and earlier ones in this book you may have found aspects of your life, relationships, or career that you wish to alter. Do not plan on making wholesale changes instantly, but choose an action, set a goal, and begin. As the old adage goes, "The Journey of a thousand miles begins with a single step." True enough. And, by the way, that journey never ends...

Where to start? A terrific way is to kill the weak first. Choose one bad habit and simply say, "That is not who I am. People like me don't do _____, we take this action instead. I will do this now and into the future."

Sounds too simple? Too easy? Actually sometimes it is! Kane has a friend who found herself becoming more and more negative as the result of a stressful job. She began taking her work frustrations out on her significant other too, which led to relationship issues. Stress at home combined with stress at work fed on each other in a vicious circle, yet one day she looked at herself in the mirror and said, "I am not that person."

To make the change she began wearing a bracelet, one she disliked. Whenever she found herself speaking or acting in a negative manner she would switch the bracelet from one wrist to another. If anyone asked, she told them why. The simple act of switching an ugly piece of jewelry from wrist to wrist helped her become keenly aware of her mindset and stop doing the destructive behaviors. After six or seven months she no longer needed the bracelet and donated it to charity.

Killing a bad habit can be simple, but sometimes, well, oftentimes it is not. Nevertheless, we argue that you should go ahead and get rid of one easy to kill habit today, right now.

What do leaders do? What is your choice? There is no timeline on this drill. Once you have successfully killed off the first bad habit or issue that has been holding you back in your leadership growth turn to the next item and go after it with knowledge of the success you just experienced. Sometimes it's easier, sometimes it's harder, but the momentum never ceases. This drill ends when they put the lid on your coffin and write your epitaph, a legacy you can be proud of.

Sensei, Mentor, Teacher, Coach – Little Life Secret:

> As a sensei, mentor, teacher, or coach you do not often get to sit in the shade of the trees that have grown from the seeds you have planted. You do get to watch them flourish nevertheless.

CONCLUSION

"Until you value yourself, you won't value your time. Until you value your time, you will not do anything with it."
M. Scott Peck[38]

The Guggenheim Museum in Manhattan New York was designed by Frank Lloyd Wright, the famous architect. Wright designed churches, skyscrapers, offices, and schools. His impression is so deep and wide that he has become a household name. Even though he passed away in 1959 his name and his legacy lives on.

Roughly 8,000 miles east of the Guggenheim is another architectural wonder, Angkor Wat. A religious complex in Cambodia, once Hindu and later repurposed as a Buddhist temple, Angkor Wat is larger than any other temple in the world. It was built in the 12th century by King Suryavarman II. Crafted of stone but interestingly without mortar, no single stone is bound to any other. Nevertheless, the complex still stands today. The greatest Roman engineers would have shaken their heads in amazement at the size and the method of building something that sophisticated.

We know who sponsored Angkor Wat, but who actually built it? The name of the architect has been lost to the winds of time. Is the genius of Angkor Wat based on the builder's name? No, but what has been left behind is a marvel nonetheless.

As Peck points out in the quote at the beginning of this section, value your time. Use it wisely, leave a sum behind, let it be good, and let it go into the future living on its own merits as you step out of the way. Follow this advice and you will have helped create a better world through your actions.

BIBLIOGRAPHY

- Abraham, Jay. *Getting Everything You can out of All You've Got: 21 Ways you can Outthink, Outperform, and Out-Earn the Competition*. New York, NY: St. Martins Press, 2000.
- Baron-Cohen, Simon. *The Essential Difference: Men, Women and the Extreme Male Brain*. New York, NY: Penguin Publishing, 2007.
- Block, Peter. *The Empowered Manager: Positive Political Skills at Work*. San Francisco, CA: Jossey-Bass Publishers, 1987.
- Cahill, Larry and Richard Haier, Nathan White, James Fallon, Lisa Kilpatrick, Chris Lawrence, Steven G. Potkin, and Michael T. Alkire. *Sex-Related Difference in Amygdala Activity during Emotionally Influenced Memory Storage*. University of California, Irvine, 2000.
- Carroll, Pete (with Yogi Roth). *Win Forever: Live, Work, and Play Like a Champion*. New York, NY; Penguin Publishing, 2010.
- Charan, Ram. *Action Urgency Excellence: Seizing Leadership in the Digital Economy*. Houston, TX: Electronic Data Systems Corp., 2000.
- Covey, Stephen M.R. and Rebecca R. Merrill. *The Speed of Trust: The one Thing that Changes Everything*. New York, NY: Simon & Schuster, 2008.
- Covey, Stephen R. and David K. Hatch. *Everyday Greatness: Inspiration for a Meaningful Live*. Nashville, TN: Thomas Nelson, 2006.
- Covey, Stephen R. *Principle-Centered Leadership*. New York, NY: Simon & Schuster, 1992.
- Covey, Stephen R. *The 7 Habits of Highly Effective People: Powerful Lessons in Personal Change*. New York, NY: Simon & Schuster, 1989.
- De Pree, Max. *Leadership is an Art*. East Lansing, MI: Michigan State University Press, 1987.
- Drucker, Peter F. *The Effective Executive*. New York, NY:

Harper & Row, 1966.
- Dungy, Tony (with Nathan Whitaker). *Quiet Strength: The Principles, Practices, and Priorities of a Winning Life*. Winter Park, FL: Legacy LLC, 2007.
- Goffee, Rob and Gareth Jones. *Why Should Anyone Be Led by You? What it Takes to Be an Authentic Leader*. Boston, MA: Harvard Business School Press, 2006.
- Grant, Adam. *Give and Take: A Revolutionary Approach to Success*. New York, NY: Viking Press, 2013.
- Greenleaf, Robert K. *The Servant as Leader*. Westfield, IN: The Greenleaf Center for Servant Leadership, 2008.
- Holmes, Stanley. Cleaning Up Boeing. *Business Week*, March 12, 2006.
- Kaye, Beverly and Sharon Jordan-Evans. *Love 'Em or Lose 'Em: Getting Good People to Stay*. San Francisco, CA: Berrett-Koehler Publishers, 1999.
- Lewis, James P. *Working Together: 12 Principles for Achieving Excellence in Managing Projects, Teams, and Organizations*. New York, NY: McGraw-Hill, 2002.
- Lombardi, Vince Jr. *The Lombardi Rules: 26 Lessons from Vince Lombardi—The World's Greatest Coach (Mighty Mangers Series)*. New York, NY: McGraw-Hill, 2003.
- Maxwell, John C. *The 21 Irrefutable Laws of Leadership: Follow Them and People Will Follow You*. Nashville, TN: Thomas Nelson, 2007.
- Maxwell, John C. *The 5 Levels of Leadership: Proven Steps to Maximize Your Potential*. New York, NY: Hachette Book Group, 2011.
- McKay, Matthew, PhD. Davis, Martha, PhD. Fanning, Patrick. *Thoughts and Feelings: Taking Control of Your Moods and Your Life*. Oakland, CA: New Harbinger Publications, Fourth Edition, 2011.
- Niednagel, Jonathan P. *Your Key to Sports Success*. Laguna Miguel, CA: Laguna Press, 1997.
- Peterson, David B. and Mary Dee Hicks. *Development First: Strategies for Self-Development*. Minneapolis, MN: Personnel Decisions International, 1995.
- Peterson, David B. and Mary Dee Hicks. *Leader as Coach: Strategies for Coaching and Developing Others*. Minneapolis,

MN: Personnel Decisions International, 1996.
- Pink, Daniel H. Drive: *The Surprising Truth about What Motivates Us*. New York, NY; Penguin Publishing, 2009.
- Pollard, C. William. *The Soul of the Firm*. New York, NY: Harper Business, 1996.
- Rath, Tom and Barry Conchie. *Strengths Based Leadership: Great Leaders, Teams, and Why People Follow*. New York, NY: Gallup Press, 2008.
- Roberts, Dan. *Unleashing the Power of IT: Bringing People, Business, and Technology Together*. Hoboken, NJ: John Wiley & Sons, 2011.
- Savage, Charles M. *5th Generation Management: Integrating Enterprises through Human Networking*. San Francisco, CA: Digital Equipment Corporation, 1990.
- Scherkenbach, William W. *The Deming Route to Quality and Productivity*. Rockville, MD: Mercury Press, 1986.
- Scott, Susan. *Fierce Conversations: Achieving Success at Work and in Life, One Conversation at a Time*. New York, NY: The Berkley Publishing Group, 2002.
- Senge, Peter M. *The Fifth Discipline: The Art and Practice of the Learning Organization*. New York, NY: Currency Doubleday, 1990.
- Treacy, Michael and Fred. Customer Intimacy and Other Value Disciplines. *Harvard Business Review*, January, 1993.
- Waddington, Tad. *Lasting Contribution: How to Think, Plan, and Act to Accomplish Meaningful Work*. Evanston, IL: Agate Publishing, 2007.
- Williamson, John N. *The Leader-Manager*. New York, NY: John Wiley & Sons, 1984.
- Wooden, John and Steve Jamison. *Wooden on Leadership: How to Create A Winning Organization*. New York, NY: McGraw-Hill, 2005.

END NOTES

1. Elbert Green Hubbard (1856 – 1915) was an American writer, publisher, artist, and philosopher. A luminary of the Arts and Crafts movement, he founded the Roycrofters artisan community in New York and published two magazines, *The Philistine* and *The Fra*. Among his many publications were the *Little Journeys to the Homes of the Great*, *The Legacy*, and the short story *A Message to Garcia* which later became a movie.
2. Winston Churchill (1874 – 1965). As prime minister of England, Sir Winston Churchill rallied the British people during WWII and led his country from the brink of defeat to victory. Working alongside U.S. President Franklin D. Roosevelt and Soviet General Secretary Joseph Stalin he was instrumental in helping the Allies defeat the Axis powers and craft post-war peace. After the post-war breakdown of the alliance, he alerted the West to the expansionist threat of Soviet Communism.
3. John Quincy Adams (1767 – 1848) was the sixth President of the United States of America. Considered one of the greatest diplomats in American history, he negotiated the Treaty of Ghent (which ended the War of 1812), the US northern border with the United Kingdom, and annexation of Florida from Spain, and authored the Monroe Doctrine.
4. Michael Jordan (1963 –) is arguably the greatest basketball player of all time. A star player for the Chicago Bulls and later the Washington Wizards, his leaping ability (illustrated primarily through slam dunks) led to the nickname Air Jordan. There is a popular line of Nike shoes that bear that name in his honor. He is currently the majority owner and chairman of the Charlotte Bobcats basketball team.
5. Excerpt of a speech given to a struggling team by Dave

Schmidt, manager of the IT Infrastructure Sourcing Strategy organization at a Fortune 50® company. He is a certified Project Management Professional (PMP) and Certified Technical Trainer (CTT+) who has published three articles through Project Management Institute (PMI). He also serves on the Board of Directors of a center that cares for drug exposed babies called Pediatric Interim Care Center (PICC) www.picc.net.

6. Al Davis (1929 – 2011) was an assistant coach, head coach, general manager, commissioner, and team owner in the National Football League. His Oakland Raiders' team motto was "Just win, baby." The Raiders played the Houston Texans the day after he passed away. Despite the fact that they only had ten players on the field, Raiders free safety Michael Huff managed to intercept Texans quarterback Matt Schaub in the end zone on the final play of the game. Dubbed the "divine interception," media pundits speculated that Davis was the 11th player on the field in spirit, leading his team to victory one final time.

7. Bill Gates (1955 –) former chief executive and current chairman of Microsoft, one the world's largest technology companies, Gates helped pioneer the personal computer industry. One of the richest men in the world, he has donated a significant portion of his income to various philanthropic efforts through his Bill and Melinda Gates Foundation and reportedly plans to give 95% of his wealth to charity.

8. Khalil Gibran (1883 – 1931) was a Lebanese artist, poet, and writer. Born in the town of Bsharri in the north of modern-day Lebanon, he immigrated with his family to the United States as a young man.

9. Rita Mae Brown (1944 –) is a novelist, screenwriter and feminist best known for her book *Rubyfruit Jungle*. Published in 1973, the novel dealt with lesbian themes in an unusually explicit manner for the time.

10. George Orwell (1903 – 1950). Born Eric Arthur Blair, but better known by his penname, Orwell was a novelist, journalist, teacher, and poet. With works that include *Nineteen Eighty Four* and *Animal Farm*, his vivid descriptions

of authoritarian regimes continue to influence popular culture long after his death, popularizing terms such as "Orwellian," "Big Brother," and "Thought Police."

11. Aristotle (384 BC – 322 BC) was a Greek philosopher and polymath. A student of Plato and teacher of Alexander the Great, Aristotle is widely considered one of the greatest philosophers of all time.
12. Walt Disney (1901 – 1966). Best known for the company that bears his name, Walter Elias "Walt" Disney was a business magnate, animator, producer, director, screenwriter, and voice actor who helped shape the entertainment industry.
13. Miguel Angel Ruiz (1952 –) better known as Don Miguel Ruiz, is a Mexican author of New Age spiritualist and neo-shamanistic texts. His most famous and influential work is *The Four Agreements*.
14. Wally is the comic creation of Scott Adams (1957 –). Famous for the *Dilbert* comic strip, Adams is the author of books such as *Always Postpone Meetings with Time-Wasting Morons*, *Dogbert's Clues for the Clueless*, *The Joy of Work*, and *Stick to Drawing Comics, Monkey Brain*. His comic creations are so popular that they can be found decorating cubicles at virtually all of the Fortune® 500 companies.
15. Mark Twain (1835 – 1910). Samuel Langhorne Clemens, better known by his pen name Mark Twain, was an author and humorist. He wrote *The Adventures of Tom Sawyer* and its sequel, *Adventures of Huckleberry Finn*, the latter often called "The Great American Novel."
16. Pearl Cleage (1948 –) is an African-American author whose works, both fiction and non-fiction, have been widely recognized. Her novel *What Looks Like Crazy on an Ordinary Day* was a 1998 Oprah Book Club selection.
17. Albert Einstein (1879 – 1955) was a German-born theoretical physicist who developed the general theory of relativity, one of the two pillars of modern physics. Awarded the Nobel Prize in Physics in 1921 for his work, Einstein emigrated from Germany to the United States in 1933. The practical applications of his theories include television sets, remote controls, lasers, and DVD-players.
18. Elizabeth Taylor (1932 – 2011). Dame Elizabeth Rosemond

"Liz" Taylor was a British-American actress who, from her early years as a child star with MGM, became one of the great screen actresses of Hollywood's Golden Age. Her famous films include *Lassie Came Home*, *The White Cliffs of Dover*, *Jane Eyre*, *National Velvet*, *Courage of Lassie*, *Giant*, *The Three Faces of Eve*, *Cat on a Hot Tin Roof*, *Suddenly Last Summer*, and *Who's Afraid of Virginia Woolf*.

19. Zig Ziglar (1926 – 2012). Hilary Hinton "Zig" Ziglar was an American author, salesman, and motivational speaker. His books include *Confessions of a Happy Christian*, *Raising Positive Kids in a Negative World*, *Success for Dummies*, *Selling 101: What Every Successful Sales Professional Needs to Know*, and *Born to Win: Find Your Success Code*.

20. Richard Bach (1936 –) is widely known as the author of the popular best-sellers *Jonathan Livingston Seagull* and *Illusions: The Adventures of a Reluctant Messiah*, among other works.

21. Vince Lombardi (1913 – 1970). One of the most successful coaches in National Football League history, Lombardi led the Green Bay Packers to five league championships in seven years. After winning the first two Super Bowls, the NFL named their Super Bowl trophy in his honor. He was enshrined in the Pro Football Hall of Fame in 1971 shortly after his death.

22. Ralph Marston is an Austin, Texas-based personal growth coach. He is the inventor and owner of, *The Daily Motivator*© website, and author of the book, *The Power of Ten Billion Dreams*.

23. Michael Jordan (1963 –) is arguably the greatest basketball player of all time. A star player for the Chicago Bulls and later the Washington Wizards, his leaping ability (illustrated primarily through slam dunks) led to the nickname Air Jordan. There is a popular line of Nike shoes that bear that name in his honor. He is currently the majority owner and chairman of the Charlotte Bobcats basketball team.

24. Robert Fripp (1946 –). Highly ranked in *Rolling Stone* magazine's list of 100 greatest guitarists of all time, Fripp is a recording musician and producer, as well as a founding

member of the progressive rock band King Crimson. He has contributed to over 700 music releases (including studio sessions, live recordings, and compilations).
25. Seneca (4 BC – 65 AD) was a Roman philosopher, statesman, and dramatist. A former tutor and advisor, he was forced to commit suicide for allegedly conspiring against the Emperor Nero.
26. Indira Priyadarshini Gandhi (1917 – 1984) was the third Prime Minister of India, the second longest serving leader of the country, and the only woman to hold the office. On the day before she was assassinated on October 30, 1984, she said, "I am alive today; I may not be there tomorrow. I shall continue to serve till my last breath and when I die every drop of my blood will strengthen India and keep a united India alive."
27. James Abbott McNeill Whistler (1834-1903) was an American artist who lived in England. He is most famous for his work "Whistlers Mother," painted in 1871.
28. W. Edwards Deming (1900 – 1993) was a statistician, professor, author, and consultant who brought the concept of continuous improvement to Japan in the 1950s. His teachings are largely responsible for Japan's innovative, high-quality products and economic prowess, typified by the Toyota Production System. He earned the United States National Medal of Technology in 1987 and received the Distinguished Career in Science award in 1988.
29. Malcolm Stevenson Forbes (1919 – 1990). At the age of 13 Malcolm obtained his first printing press and by the age of 15 he had published papers for his household, the Scouts, and school. He became the owner and publisher of the *Fairfield Times* newspaper only days after his graduation from Princeton. He went on to publish the *Lancaster Tribune* in 1942, and after a stint in the army on the European front during World War II, he joined the staff at *Forbes Magazine* where he eventually became its publisher.
30. Elisabeth Kübler-Ross, M.D. (1926 -2004) was a psychologist who pioneered the field of near-death studies. Her 1969 book, *On Death and Dying*, first discussed the widely-acknowledged theory of the five stages of grief.

31. Theodore "Teddy" Roosevelt (1858 – 1919), organized a volunteer cavalry known as the "Rough Riders" during the Spanish-American War. Nominated for a Congressional Medal of Honor for his heroic role in the Battle of San Juan Heights, he leveraged his fame to get elected Governor of New York and subsequently Vice President of the United States. At age 42, he became the youngest man to assume the U.S. presidency following the assassination of President William McKinley in 1901, and won a second term in 1904. Known for his anti-monopoly policies and ecological conservationism, Roosevelt won the Nobel Peace Prize for his part in ending the Russo-Japanese War.
32. Lido Anthony "Lee" Iacocca (1924 –) is an auto industry executive and author. After engineering the Ford Mustang and Pinto he was let go from Ford Motor Company and then famously brought back into the car industry to revive the failing Chrysler Corporation. He served as President and CEO of Chrysler from 1978 and additionally as chairman from 1979 until his retirement in 1992. He is the author of several books, including *Iacocca: An Autobiography* (with William Novak), and *Where Have All the Leaders Gone?*
33. Tom Peters (1942 –) is an American author, businessman, and consultant, best known for his book *In Search of Excellence*.
34. Sun Tzu (544–496 BC) is an honorific that means "Master Sun." According to historians, his given name was Wu. His mastery of military strategy was so exceptional that he supposedly transformed 180 courtesans into trained soldiers in a single session in order to secure a generalship with King Ho-Lu. Whether that particular episode is true or not it is well known King Ho-Lu, with Sun Tzu at his side, defeated the powerful Chinese Ch'u state in 506 BC, capturing their capital city of Ying. He then headed north and subdued the states of Ch'i and Chin to forge his empire. Sun Tzu recorded his winning strategies in a book titled *The Art of War*. It was the first and most revered volume of its type, one that is still referenced by military and business leaders throughout the world today.

35. It is unclear where this quote first originated, versions of this have been used by many famous individuals including Dale Carnegie, but it is often attributed to Paul White, the first director of CBS radio news. It has been referred to as the White Formula for radio news reporting.
36. Colin Luther Powell (1937 –) is a retired United States Army Four-star General. Powell began his leadership journey by joining the army's Reserve Officers' Training Corps (ROTC) while attending City College in New York. He eventually went on to serve as Chairman of the Joint Chiefs of Staff and as the 65th United States Secretary of State.
37. Coach Darin Slack is the founder and president of the National Football Academies (www.nationalfootballacademies.com), a football camp development and training program active in over 80 cities, with over 200 certified coaches whose passion is to coach football and build men. It is the largest quarterback-specific training organization in the world. Prior to founding NFA, Coach Slack was a standout athlete at the University of Central Florida where he set many school records as a quarterback.
38. Morgan Scott Peck (1936 –2005) was an American psychiatrist and best-selling author, best known for his first book, *The Road Less Traveled*.

About the Authors

Lawrence A. Kane:

Lawrence is a senior leader at a Fortune® 50 corporation where he architected the IT infrastructure strategy, governed the software asset management process, and established the Sourcing Strategy & Vendor Management competency center. He saved the company well over $1.8B by hiring, training, and developing a high-performance team that creates sourcing strategies, improves processes, negotiates contracts, and benchmarks internal and external supplier performance. He previously worked as a business technology instructor at a technical college for eight years where received student accolades for communicating effectively, demonstrating patience, and fostering a positive learning environment.

He is the best-selling author of nine books, including an *eLit Book Awards* Bronze prize, a *Next Generation Indie Book Awards* finalist, two *USA Book News* Best Books Award finalists, and two *ForeWord Magazine* Book of the Year Award finalists. A founding technical consultant to University of New Mexico's Institute of Traditional Martial Arts, he also has written numerous articles on martial arts, self-defense, countervailing force, and related topics. He has spoken with journalists numerous times, including once where he was interviewed in English by a reporter from a Swiss newspaper for an article that was published in French, and found that oddly amusing.

Since 1970, he has studied and taught traditional Asian martial arts, medieval European combat, and modern close-quarter weapon techniques. Working stadium security part-time for 26 years he was involved in hundreds of violent altercations, but got paid to watch football.

Lawrence lives in Seattle, Washington with his son Joey and wife Julie. You can contact him directly at lakane@ix.netcom.com.

Kris Wilder:

Kris Wilder is the head instructor and owner of West Seattle Karate Academy. He started practicing the martial arts at the age of fifteen. Over the years he has earned black belt rankings in three styles, *Goju-Ryu* karate (5th *dan*), tae kwon do (2nd *dan*), and judo (1st *dan*), in which he has competed in senior nationals and international tournaments. He is the author of eight books including two *USA Book News* Best Books Award finalists and a *ForeWord Magazine* Book of the Year Award finalist. He also stars in two instructional DVDs.

He is a co-host of *Martial Secrets* (which can be found at www.martial-Secrets.com or on iTunes), a bi-weekly podcast with his frequent co-author Lawrence Kane which covers a wide range of subjects regarding martial arts, self-protection, and even a little humor. Kris also hosts *Life and Martial Arts*, a bi-weekly podcast that deals with deeper subjects spanning, life, action, self-actualization, and contemplation that can be found at www.kriswilder.com/category/podcasts/.

Kris has been blessed with the opportunity to train under skilled instructors, including Olympic athletes, state champions, national champions, and gifted martial artists who take their lineage directly from the founders of their systems. He teaches seminars worldwide, focusing on growing a person's martial technique and their understanding, whatever their art may be. Kris also serves as a National Representative for the University of New Mexico's Institute of Traditional Martial Arts.

Kris spent about 15 years in the political and public affairs area, working for campaigns from the local to national level. During this consulting career he was periodically on staff for elected officials. His work also involved lobbying and corporate affairs. He is currently a member of The Order of St. Francis (OSF); the OSF is one of many active Apostolic Christian Orders.

Kris lives in Seattle, Washington with his son Jackson. You can contact him directly at thedojo@quidnunc.net.

OTHER WORKS BY THE AUTHORS

Non-Fiction Books:

1. ***Dirty Ground*** (Kane/Wilder)

   "Fills a void in martial arts training." – Loren W. Christensen, Martial Arts Masters Hall of Fame member

   This book addresses a significant gap in most martial arts training, the tricky space that lies between sport and combat applications when you need to control a person without injuring him (or her). Techniques in this region are called "drunkle," named after the drunken uncle disrupting a family gathering. Understanding how to deal with combat, sport, and drunkle situations is vital because appropriate use of force is codified in law and actions that do not accommodate these regulations can have severe repercussions. Martial arts techniques must be adapted to best fit the situation you find yourself in. This book shows you how.

2. ***How to Win a Fight*** (Kane/Wilder)

   "It is the ultimate course in self-defense and will help you survive and get through just about any violent situation or attack." – Jeff Rivera, bestselling author

   More than three million Americans are involved in a violent physical encounter every year. Develop the fortitude to walk away when you can and prevail when you must. Defense begins by scanning your environment, recognizing hazards and escape routes, and using verbal de-escalation to defuse tense situations. If a fight is unavoidable, the authors offer clear guidance for being the victor, along with advice on legal implications, including how to handle a police interview after the attack.

3. *Lessons from the Dojo Floor* (Wilder)

"Helps each reader, from white belt to black belt, look at and understand why he or she trains." – Michael E. Odell, Isshin-Ryu Northwest Okinawa Karate Association

In the vein of Dave Lowry, a thought provoking collection of short vignettes that entertains while it educates. Packed with straightforward, easy, and quick to read sections that range from profound to insightful to just plain amusing, anyone with an affinity for martial arts can benefit from this material.

4. *Martial Arts Instruction* (Kane)

"Boeing trains hundreds of security officers, Kane's ideas will help us be more effective." – Gregory A. Gwash, Chief Security Officer, Boeing

While the old adage, "those who can't do, teach," is not entirely true, all too often "those who can do" cannot teach effectively. This book is unique in that it offers a holistic approach to teaching martial arts; incorporating elements of educational theory and communication techniques typically overlooked in budo (warrior arts). Teachers will improve their abilities to motivate, educate, and retain students, while students interested in the martial arts will develop a better understanding of what instructional method best suits their needs.

5. *Scaling Force* (Kane/Miller)

"If you're serious about learning how the application of physical force works—before, during and after the fact—I cannot recommend this book highly enough."
– Lieutenant Jon Lupo, New York State Police

Conflict and violence cover a broad range of behaviors, from intimidation to murder, and require an equally broad range of responses. A kind word will not resolve all situations, nor will wristlocks, punches, or even a gun. This book introduces the full range of options, from skillfully doing nothing to employing deadly force. You will understand the limits of each type of force, when specific levels may be appropriate, the circumstances under which you may have to apply them, and the potential costs, legally and personally, of your decision.

6. *Surviving Armed Assaults* (Kane)

"This book will be an invaluable resource for anyone walking the warrior's path, and anyone who is interested in this vital topic." – Lt. Col. Dave Grossman, Director, Warrior Science Group

A sad fact is that weapon-wielding thugs victimize 1,773,000 citizens every year in the United States alone. Even martial artists are not immune from this deadly threat. Consequently, self-defense training that does not consider the very real possibility of an armed attack is dangerously incomplete. Whether you live in the city or countryside, you should be both mentally and physically prepared to deal with an unprovoked armed assault at any time. Preparation must be comprehensive enough to account for the plethora of pointy objects, blunt instruments, explosive devices, and deadly projectiles that someday could be used against you. This extensive book teaches proven survival skills that can keep you safe.

7. **The Little Black Book of Violence** (Kane/Wilder)

"This book will save lives!" – Alain Burrese, JD, former US Army 2nd Infantry Division Scout Sniper School instructor

Men commit 80 % of all violent crimes and are twice as likely to become the victims of aggressive behavior. This book is primarily written for men ages 15 to 35, and contains more than mere self-defense techniques. You will learn crucial information about street survival that most martial arts instructors don't even know. Discover how to use awareness, avoidance, and de-escalation to help stave off violence, know when it's prudent to fight, and understand how to do so effectively.

8. **The Way of Kata** (Kane/Wilder)

"This superb book is essential reading for all those who wish to understand the highly effective techniques, concepts, and strategies that the kata were created to record." – Iain Abernethy, British Combat Association Hall of Fame member

The ancient masters developed kata, or "formal exercises," as fault-tolerant methods to preserve their unique, combat-proven fighting systems. Unfortunately, they also deployed a two-track system of instruction where an outer circle of students unknowingly received modified forms with critical details or important principles omitted. Only the select inner circle that had gained a master's trust and respect would be taught okuden waza, the powerful hidden applications of kata. The theory of deciphering kata applications (kaisai no genri) was once a great mystery revealed only to trusted disciples of the ancient masters in order to protect the secrets of their systems. Even today, while the basic movements of kata are widely known, advanced practical applications and sophisticated techniques frequently remain hidden from the casual observer. The principles and rules for understanding kata are largely unknown. This groundbreaking book unveils these methods, not only teaching you how to analyze your kata to understand what it is trying to tell you, but also helping you to utilize your fighting techniques more effectively.

9. **The Way of Martial Arts for Kids** (Wilder)

"Written in a personable, engaging style that will appeal to kids and adults alike." – Laura Weller, Guitarist, The Green Pajamas

Based on centuries of traditions, martial arts training can be a positive experience for kids. The book helps you and yours get the most out of class. It shows how just about any child can become one of those few exemplary learners who excel in the training hall as well as in life. Written to children, it is also for parents too. After all, while the martial arts instructor knows his art, no one knows his/her child better than the parent. Together you can help your child achieve just about anything… The advice provided is straightforward, easy to understand, and written with a child-reader in mind so that it can either be studied by the child and/or read together with the parent.

10. **The Way of Sanchin Kata** (Wilder)

"This book has been sorely needed for generations!" – Philip Starr, National Chairman, Yiliquan Martial Arts Association

When Karate or Ti was first developed in Okinawa it was about using technique and extraordinary power to end a fight instantly. These old ways of generating remarkable power are still accessible, but they are purposefully hidden in Sanchin kata for the truly dedicated to find. This book takes the practitioner to new depths of practice by breaking down the form piece-by-piece, body part by body part, so that the very foundation of the kata is revealed. Every chapter, concept, and application is accompanied by a "Test It" section, designed for you to explore and verify the kata for yourself. Sanchin kata really comes alive when you feel the thrill of having those hidden teachings speak to you across the ages through your body. Simply put, once you read this book and test what you have learned, your karate will never be the same.

11. *The Way to Black Belt* (Kane/Wilder)

"*It is so good I wish I had written it myself.*" – Hanshi Patrick McCarthy, Director, International Ryukyu Karate Research Society

Cut to the very core of what it means to be successful in the martial arts. Earning a black belt can be the most rewarding experience of a lifetime, but getting there takes considerable planning. Whether your interests are in the classical styles of Asia or in today's Mixed Martial Arts, this book prepares you to meet every challenge. Whatever your age, whatever your gender, you will benefit from the wisdom of master martial artists around the globe, including Iain Abernethy, Dan Anderson, Loren Christensen, Jeff Cooper, Wim Demeere, Aaron Fields, Rory Miller, Martina Sprague, Phillip Starr, and many more, who share more than 300 years of combined training experience. Benefit from their guidance during your development into a first-class black belt.

Fiction Books:

1. ***Blinded by the Night*** (Kane)

    "Kane's expertise in matters of mayhem shines throughout." – Steve Perry, bestselling author

    Richard Hayes is a Seattle cop. After 25 years with the PD he thinks he knows everything there is to know about predators. The dregs of society like rapists, murderers, gang bangers, and child molesters are just another day at the office. Commonplace criminals become the least of his problems when he goes hunting for a serial killer and runs into a real monster. The creature not only attacks him, but merely gets pissed off when he shoots it. In the head. Twice! Surviving that fight is only the beginning. Richard discovers that the vampire he destroyed was the ruler of an eldritch realm he never dreamed existed. By some archaic rule, having defeated the monster's sovereign in battle, Richard becomes their new king. Now he is responsible for a host of horrors who stalk the night, howl at the moon, and shamble through the darkness. But, why would these creatures willingly obey a human? When it comes to human predators, Richard is a seasoned veteran, yet with paranormal ones he is but a rookie. He must navigate a web of intrigue and survive long enough to discover how a regular guy can tangle with supernatural creatures and prevail. One mistake and things surely won't end well...

DVDs:

1. ***121 Killer Appz*** (Wilder/Kane)

    "Quick and brutal, the way karate is meant to be." – Eric Parsons, Founder, Karate for Life Foundation
    You know the kata, now it is time for the applications.

Gekisai (Dai Ni), Saifa, Seiyunchin, Seipai, Kururunfa, Suparinpei, Sanseiru, Shisochin, and Seisan kata are covered. If you ever wondered what purpose a move from a Goju Ryu karate form was for, wonder no longer. This DVD contains no discussion, just a no-nonsense approach to one application after another. It is sure to provide deeper understanding to your kata practice and stimulate thought on determining your own applications to the Goju Ryu karate forms.

2. *Sanchin Kata: Three Battles Karate Kata* (Wilder)

"A cornucopia of martial arts knowledge." – Shawn Kovacich, endurance high-kicking world record holder (as certified by the Guinness Book of World Records)

A traditional training method for building karate power Sanchin kata, or Three Battles Sequence, is an ancient form that can be traced back to the roots of karate. Some consider it the missing link between Chinese kung fu and Okinawan karate. Sanchin kata is known to develop extraordinary quickness and generate remarkable power. This program breaks down the form piece by piece, body part by body part, so that the hidden details of the kata are revealed. Regular practice of Sanchin kata conditions the body, trains correct alignment, and teaches the essential structure needed for generating power within all of your karate movements. Many karate practitioners believe that Sanchin kata holds the key to mastering the traditional martial arts. Though it can be one of the simplest forms to learn, it is simultaneously one of the most difficult to perfect. This DVD complements the book *The Way of Sanchin Kata*, providing in-depth exploration of the form, with detailed instruction of the essential posture, linking the spine, generating power, and demonstration of the complete kata.

Made in the USA
San Bernardino, CA
18 March 2014